Dec 19/72

to Hays Lloyd
with my thanks
and best wishes

Pat Morley.

THE IMMORAL MORALISTS

Clarke, Irwin & Company Limited / TORONTO / VANCOUVER / 1972

Hugh MacLennan and Leonard Cohen

THE IMMORAL MORALISTS

Patricia A. Morley

© 1972 by Clarke, Irwin & Company Limited

ISBN 0-7720-0555-9 (Hardbound)
ISBN 7720-0581-8 (Paperback)

Printed in Canada

This study is dedicated to all
Canadian puritans:
Here's to us!
Wha's like us?

PREFACE

Several years ago it occurred to me that the novels of two Canadian writers a generation apart from each other could be juxtaposed in order to highlight cultural changes in Canada in the last twenty-five years. MacLennan and Cohen seemed the obvious choice. And so began this para-literary study which cuts across such related disciplines as religion, history, and literature. I would like to thank Dr. Robert McDougall for discussions in 1967 on Hugh MacLennan's fiction; the Reverend Ronald Rowat and Professor Alex McGregor for contributing to my understanding of Calvinism; and Mrs. Margaret Pelton for typing the manuscript.

There is, of course, a danger in making use of novels and poetry as social documents, since the former are works of art whose meaning lies in the statement made by the work as a whole and in the relationship of its parts. I am aware of this danger, and of the possible fallacy of equating Cohen's or MacLennan's ideas with those of their fictional characters. The danger can be reduced, if not entirely eliminated, by considering the total context of the fictional evidence. Most literary criticism assumes that this is possible.

MacLennan and Cohen write of Canada *from the inside*, as artists must do. I also write of Canada, and of the work of Canadian novelists, from the inside. I am a Canadian, born and bred in Toronto, a lifelong resident of Ontario. The experience of travelling in other countries and studying other cultures has added to my understanding of what it is to be a Canadian. I am the product of a Protestant background and a puritan atmosphere (although mine, I hasten to add, was not nearly so rigid as that of MacLennan's Broughton or Grenville). Like MacLennan, I claim an insider's knowledge of this tradition. My stance, as a literary critic of his work, is inevitably different from that of, say, a Japanese critic who has become fluent in the English language. Education enables us to transcend our experience to a certain degree; but education also leads us to the realization that our original cultural heritage is never completely transcended. Both novelist and critic operate within traditions (literary, social, religious, and so on) and not in a cultural vacuum. Honesty seems to require this admission.

Age is also a factor. I belong to Cohen's generation. I have seen my own attitudes changed or modified in the last twenty years through the influence of changing cultural forces. MacLennan's work now spans two generations, it being thirty years since the publication of *Barometer Rising*, his first novel. We find a change in his attitude toward sexual mores, for example, in his latest novels. Even more noticeable (for an artist is usually in advance of his times) is the difference in public reaction to sexuality in MacLennan's work now, compared with thirty years ago.

I hope, finally, that my study may contribute to the re-evaluation of that much-abused word *puritan*. Simone Weil reminds us of our need for roots, while MacLennan terms the present generation a psychic orphan. I suggest that we look to our religious heritage to rediscover our roots.

Patricia A. Morley
Manotick, Ontario
September 1972

EDITIONS CITED

Throughout the book, parenthetical reference will often be made after a quote to one of the following books. The abbreviated title will be used. All page references to the works of Hugh MacLennan and Leonard Cohen are to the editions cited below.

MacLennan, Hugh

- *Barometer Rising* (1941). Intro. Hugo McPherson, NCL 8. Toronto: McClelland and Stewart, 1961. / *BR*
- *Two Solitudes.* New York: Duell, Sloan & Pearce, 1945. / *TS*
- *The Precipice.* Toronto: Collins, 1948. / *P*
- *Each Man's Son* (1951). Intro. Alec Lucas, NCL 30. Toronto: McClelland and Stewart, 1962. / *EMS*
- *The Watch That Ends the Night.* Toronto: Macmillan, 1959. / *WE*
- *Return of the Sphinx.* Toronto: Macmillan, 1967. / *RS*
- *Cross Country.* Toronto: Collins, 1949. / *CC*
- *Thirty and Three.* Toronto: Macmillan, 1954. / *T & T*
- *Scotchman's Return and Other Essays.* Toronto: Macmillan, 1960. / *SR*

Cohen, Leonard

- *The Favorite Game* (1963). New York: Avon, 1965. / *FG*
- *Beautiful Losers.* Toronto: McClelland and Stewart, 1966. / *BL*

CONTENTS

ACKNOWLEDGEMENTS

The author and publisher wish to thank the following companies and individuals for permission to quote from their works: Coles Publishing Company Limited (*Hugh MacLennan*, by Peter Buitenhuis, Forum House); J. M. Dent & Sons (Canada) Limited (*Puritanism and Liberty*, by A. S. P. Woodhouse, J. M. Dent & Sons (Canada) Limited); Mr. Robert Fulford and *The Toronto Star* ("A wave of absurdist fiction . . . ," "Face Off . . . ," "Canadian no real emotional sense . . . ," all by Robert Fulford, Reprinted with permission Toronto Star); *The Globe and Mail* ("Colourful recall in an artist's book," by Kay Kritzwiser, *The Globe and Mail*, Dec. 9, 1970; "Observing the Swinging Explosion," by William French, *Globe Magazine*, April 10, 1971); Harcourt Brace Jovanovich, Inc. (*Religion and the Rise of Capitalism*, by R. H. Tawney, Harcourt Brace); Harper and Row (*The Puritans*, by P. Miller and T. H. Johnson, Harper and Row); Hugh MacLennan and *The Gazette* ("Murder of truth . . . murder of people," by Hugh Mac-Lennan, *The Gazette*, Nov. 21, 1970); The Macmillan Company of Canada Limited (*Each Man's Son, Return of the Sphinx*, both by Hugh MacLennan, The Macmillan Company of Canada Limited); McGraw-Hill Ryerson Limited (Reprinted from *On Canadian Poetry* by E. K. Brown, The Ryerson Press, by permission of McGraw-Hill Ryerson Limited); M. Eugene Osterhaven; *The Toronto Star* ("Keep it Canadian . . . ," by John Doig, *The Toronto Star*, Dec. 1971, Reprinted with permission Toronto Star); *The Toronto Star* (the cartoon, reproduced with permission Toronto Star).

The book has been published with the help of a grant from the Social Science Research Council of Canada, using funds provided by the Canada Council.

".... hey buddy ... buy a set of chaste postcards ... fully clothed maidens in sedate poses ... be a leader in the coming swing back to puritanism ..."

1 THE PURITAN HERITAGE

MacLennan pictures our generation as an orphan, a psychic waif, isolated from his cultural heritage by war, science and technology. The narrator of Cohen's *Beautiful Losers* describes history as a burden he cannot carry any longer. Canadians have found themselves, since World War II, in a period of rapid cultural change. In the social, political and psychic turbulence of the sixties, changes seemed to centre in attitudes towards work, sexual relationships and the pursuit of pleasure. These are the very areas involved in MacLennan's definition of puritanism. An analysis of the fiction of Hugh MacLennan and Leonard Cohen reveals some of the implications of these changes. I find the works of both authors curiously representative, in many ways, of Canadian attitudes. The similarities between the personal values of these two writers, as affirmed by their fiction, are as significant as their differences.

Cohen was born in 1934; MacLennan, in 1907. Certain modifications in MacLennan's ideas over the three decades covered by his fiction can be seen by comparing his first four novels with his fifth and sixth. We may study the changes in Canadian social patterns in these three decades by juxtaposing the way in which subjects such as work, sex and enjoyment are treated in the fiction of these two writers. MacLennan's first four novels were published between 1941 and 1951. In these, he shows us Canadian pre-war convictions, some of which had suffered remarkably little change for many generations, being subjected to the stress of changing attitudes in the forties.

While it is difficult to define historic traditions accurately, I cannot agree with those who consider tradition to be only a matter for speculation. Changing attitudes, moreover, do not necessarily mean an outright denial of earlier beliefs. Moral values are subject to continual reassessment, and iconoclasts often claim, with good reason, to be attempting (like the historic Puritans) to recover the purity of an old ideal. Both MacLennan and Cohen are religious writers: moralists, idealists, truth-seekers. Sometimes mystics. MacLennan, like many Canadians, inherited a religious culture based on the Christianity which emerged from the religious upheavals in Europe in the sixteenth and seventeenth centuries. He is marked, to a greater extent than he has yet acknowledged, by the strengths and affirmations of that historic Puritanism. Cohen inherits Jewish religious ideals. Classical Judaism is, like historic Puritanism, both moralistic and rationalistic.[1] In his novels, Cohen, like MacLennan, seems to reject the institutional form of his religion, while affirming many of its basic ideals.

It is necessary for Canadians to understand the relationship between our Puritan past and our present violent reaction to this heritage. The moral climate which has come to prevail in Canada in the last twenty-five years is very different from the pre-war attitudes depicted in MacLennan's first four novels. He has chosen to denounce many of these earlier practices as "puritan." And the word, in MacLennan's mouth, is no compliment. In his novels and essays, MacLennan attacks puritanism as negative, pernicious. He condemns the puritan emphasis on action as materialistic. MacLennan's puritan is a person ridden with feelings of guilt, driven to work compulsively, and severed from the enjoyment of beauty and pleasure.

It is an attractive thesis, and one that many of us have bought in the last few decades. I was a fellow-traveller for a time. Then I began to realize that the creative self-discipline and restraint that distinguished many Canadians was largely puritan in origin. Nor is this characteristic as easily disassociated from its religious roots as MacLennan sometimes suggests. Certain aspects of historic Puritanism are considered in Chapter Three. The negative attitude which MacLennan deplores can be found among the more extreme of the historic Puritan groups. Seventeenth-century Puritanism, however, is characterized most strongly by a religious fervour and a moral idealism. The Puritan emphasis on action was not negative in its original intention. Believing that "faith without works is dead," the Puritan dedicated his labours to the service of God.

Puritanism, in MacLennan's definition, has no necessary connection with Protestantism. Some of the ideas generated by the Protestant Reformation were embodied in Roman Catholicism through the Counter-Reformation. In *Two Solitudes*, MacLennan depicts the Roman Catholic priest of the parish of Saint-Marc as puritan. In his essay "Cross Country," he emphasizes that puritans need not belong to any Christian denomination or indeed to any religious tradition: "Whether midwesterners go to church on Sundays or stay at home to read the comics in steam-heated apartments makes no difference for puritanism is a state of mind no more fundamental to religion than a coat of barnacles is fundamental to the keel of a ship."

Historically, the narrow puritanism of MacLennan's definition had its origin partly in Protestant Calvinism and partly in Catholic Jansenism. Norah Story writes that the followers of Cornelius Jansen preached a Calvinistic doctrine based on predestination; and that the doctrine was bitterly opposed by the Jesuits (who were preeminent in the province of Quebec). Nevertheless, Story writes, Jansenism "introduced a strong puritan note that influenced clergy who remained untouched by Jansenist doctrines. This type of puritanism became a characteristic of French-Canadian Catholicism."[2] Monasticism, the celibacy of the Roman clergy, and the various manifestations of the Manichaean heresy which are always current have also played a part in Christianity's ascetic tradition. What MacLennan calls puritan is not synonymous with the historic phenomenon of Puritanism nor with the Canadian heritage. But *many* Canadians, whether their origins be Scottish, United Empire Loyalist, or French Catholic, have emerged from this Puritan tradition, either in its stricter or more liberal versions. And *all* have felt its influence in a host of ways ranging from laws governing the observance of Sunday, or standards of dress and decorum, to the high priorities our nation sets upon education.

Let us examine, first, MacLennan's definition of the word. Puritanism, in MacLennan's work, represents an entirely negative complex of ideas and attitudes. He sees it as "an ancient curse," deeply engrained in the Canadian and American character, and he writes to help us rid ourselves of the blight. Believing that the substance of any living literature comes out of the society to which the writer belongs, and that the ideal reader must share the writer's cultural heritage or be brought to share in it by the writer's power of communication, he hopes that his writing may help us to understand ourselves and to shed the puritan incubus. He does not stand alone in this. Many post-war writers have condemned puritanism as evil and repressive.

There are those who do not agree with MacLennan's definition of puritanism as an ancient curse, yet who share his conviction that puritanism is a basic component of the Canadian character. It is necessary to understand puritanism in order to understand North

America. The popular conception of the word today is close to Mac-Lennan's. Like him, the man on the street associates the word with negation and repression. But when the religious and ethical implications are examined and the historic background considered, Mac-Lennan's definition cannot go unchallenged.

In his Introduction to *The Puritans: A Sourcebook of Their Writings*, Perry Miller notes that historic Puritanism is more easily described than defined: "It figures frequently in controversy of the last decade, very seldom twice with exactly the same connotation. Particularly of recent years, it has become a hazardous feat to run down its meaning. In the mood of revolt against the ideals of previous generations which has swept over our period, Puritanism has become a shining target for many sorts of marksmen."[3]

Many others testify to the difficulties of defining puritanism. It was in England in the 1560's that the advocates of church reform first acquired the name of Puritans. In the century following, the connotations of the word were much more definite than they are now, although even in the seventeenth century there was a tremendous variety in the beliefs and attitudes of Puritans. These beliefs, in the following centuries, were subject to constant alterations and reinterpretations. In many cases, the original positive intention was lost, and only a negative perversion of the original idea remained. In our own century there is an emotional aura attached to the word which makes an objective study of historic Puritanism difficult, and a general consensus on a current definition almost impossible. It can become a handy term of opprobrium for almost anything of which one disapproves.

Although the meaning of puritanism varies with the writer, it is not difficult to reach an understanding of the meaning which Mac-Lennan attaches to the word. From his essays and from his first four novels there emerges a clear and consistent picture which is best summed up in the phrase from the Author's Note to *Each Man's Son* – an ancient curse:

> To Cape Breton the Highlanders brought . . . an ancient curse, intensified by John Calvin and branded upon their souls by John Knox and his successors – the belief that man has inherited from Adam a nature so sinful there is no hope for him and that, furthermore, he lives and dies under the wrath of an arbitrary God who will forgive only a handful of His elect on the Day of Judgment. . . . So the curse remained alive with them, like a somber beast growling behind an unlocked door. It was felt even when they were least conscious of it. To escape its cold breath some turned to drink and others to the pursuit of knowledge. . . .

Daniel Ainslie was one of those who stayed. . . . But he did not know – how many of us can understand such a thing – that every day of his life was haunted by a sense of sin, a legacy of the ancient curse.

The central significance in the term as MacLennan uses it is the sense of sin and accompanying guilt feelings. This conviction, in those blighted by puritanism, underlies all feelings and results in a basic inability to enjoy life. MacLennan thus equates puritanism with a death-wish, and one of the structural principles in his fiction is the confrontation between these death-seeking attitudes labelled "puritan" and the belief that life is something vital and joyous to be accepted with gratitude and enjoyed to the full. The latter is represented most clearly by Catherine in *The Watch That Ends the Night* and by Constance in *Return of the Sphinx.*

MacLennan sees guilt as the legacy of puritanism. It operates to inhibit enjoyment and to deny individual self-fulfilment. The puritanism which he attacks has lost its understanding of the religious *reasons* for its commands and prohibitions; there remains only a diffused suspicion or outright rejection of beauty and pleasure and joy. The puritan tends to be afraid of his own emotions, as Bruce and Lucy find in *The Precipice*: "Generations of Calvinism had made them all afraid of themselves. The great emotions, love and fear and hate and desire, could break like thunderclaps in his mind as in hers, and because of their training they would both try to conceal them with matter-of-fact words or a quick change of subject." The guilt which puritanism has come to associate with beauty, emotion and joy has been extended to man's sexual nature; puritanism considers the sexual act as sinful, or indeed as the chief sin. This puritan attitude is personified by Jane who, as Grenville's collective conscience, believes that sex is "the dirtiest thing in the world, and near to the root of all evil."

The final important characteristic of puritanism in MacLennan's definition is an irrational and obsessive compulsion to work. In *Each Man's Son,* Dr. Ainslie turns to his self-imposed study of Greek after he has exhausted himself at the hospital. He refuses to rest, refuses to allow himself to enjoy life. His wife realizes that he actually fears rest and enjoyment because of his feelings of guilt.

A rejection of beauty and pleasure, a condemnation of man's sexual nature, and a compulsion to work: this is the essence of puritanism as MacLennan sees it. The puritan, failing in these self-imposed standards, is plagued with guilt, shame and fear. MacLennan emphasizes that the sense of guilt may continue in generations which have ceased to have any religious faith. The original theological basis for guilt is replaced by conditioned reflexes built into the emotions. MacLennan's characters frequently judge and condemn themselves and seem unable to accept their own weaknesses or sin.

Here one senses a strange deficiency in MacLennan's understanding of Christianity: an inability to recognize that its concern with guilt is paralleled and balanced by its belief in the opportunity for forgiveness and the certainty of God's mercy. A very strict Calvinistic interpretation of predestination is apparently the reason for MacLennan's treatment of guilt. In his determination to free the individual from its paralysing effects, he seems to suggest an outright denial of the existence of moral guilt as the only solution, whereas the traditional Christian solution has emphasized the remission, not the denial, of sin. In his essays, MacLennan has said that contemporary puritanism has no connection with religion at all. Under his own definition of the term, this is quite valid. But in his novels, at least when dealing with characters who are Protestant Christians, MacLennan still treats the problem of guilt as one with no apparent *religious* solution. In *Each Man's Son*, Ainslie's experience of release from guilt has no relation to his Presbyterian religion. In *The Precipice*, Marcia has to become a Roman Catholic before MacLennan can allow her to feel forgiven; and the feeling of absolution which MacLennan suggests *may* be achieved by Stephen has no relation to any religious faith. This strange inability of his characters to experience forgiveness seems basic to MacLennan's idea of puritanism and helps to explain his antagonism to it. The paralysing effects of guilt are emphasized in *The Precipice* through the character of Stephen. In the last chapter, Lucy thinks that Stephen, even when drunk and in bed with another woman, is more of a puritan than she herself has ever been. And this is because he feels guilty.

Whereas the novels clothe in flesh and blood MacLennan's conception of puritanism as negative and repressive, his essays name and attack it directly. Speaking of the Canadian character in *Cross Country*, MacLennan writes of the success which established religion in Canada has had in curbing exuberances: "The authority of the Quebec priest over his parish is famous. In the English-speaking provinces, Calvinism has been endemic from the beginning. Although both religions have done much to fortify Canadian society in the face of geographical debits, they have enormously inhibited the Canadian character in the process." More than once in this collection of essays, MacLennan reaffirms the connection between Calvinist and Jansenist puritanism and deep-rooted inhibitions in the Canadian character. He claims that Americans are proud of what they *do* while Canadians are proud of what they *don't* do. It is an interesting summary of MacLennan's ideas on what puritanism involves, with Americans representing the compulsion to work, and Canadians, the denial of beauty, joy and sex.

The puritan compulsion to work and act is condemned by Mac-Lennan as materialistic. In "Cross Country," MacLennan is speaking of puritanism as the dominating influence on the prosperous middle classes of the northern and midwestern United States.[4] This is one of the rare occasions on which MacLennan allows the word "puritan" to stand for any strength or virtue. He writes: "The middle classes of this part of the United States have the strengths and weaknesses of puritans everywhere. They are tremendously industrious, competent, hard-headed, practical, and courageous. On the other hand, they understand internal combustion engines better than they understand themselves, and they trust efficient organization more than they trust human nature." This is the single exception to the totally negative meaning which MacLennan chooses to associate with the word puritanism. I hope to demonstrate that Puritanism in the seventeenth century did indeed have both strengths and weaknesses, especially strengths, and that many of its more positive characteristics are to be found in MacLennan himself. Only in this one essay, however, has MacLennan credited the puritan with any virtues – and they are the sort of virtues admired by Ben Franklin. After this concession, MacLennan condemns the puritan for being uninterested in mystery, intolerant of weakness, fearful of failure, and totally ignorant of human nature.

In the same essay he says that America's crisis has come about because puritanism "conditioned its members to act rather than to think, to deal with means rather than ends, to press forward with ever-increasing speed toward a material goal." A few pages later, he speaks of the "materialistic panacea" of the puritans and the "puritan conception that what a man does can be separated from what a man is." Here and elsewhere, he links puritanism with the evils of mass production and all the materialistic associations of the world of George Babbitt. He opposes this to the European heritage, a "priceless" cultural heritage which the puritan is unable to appreciate.

Writing in defence of D.H. Lawrence, MacLennan says that the ethic of Lawrence is in direct opposition to the one which permeates our materialistic society, where the chief purpose is to produce, distribute and consume. Human individuality is as dangeous to such a society as a fifth column: "So is the human spirit, which must take a secondary place to the demands of the I.B.M. machine or the assembly line." The ideals of individualism and of freedom for the human spirit are clearly affirmed in both his novels and essays, and he attacks puritanism for preventing the individual's full development and freedom of spirit.

In the collection of essays called *Thirty and Three*, MacLennan speaks of the "negative shibboleths and taboos" of puritan morality. Sometimes he uses "Scotch" as a loose synonym for Calvinist, and hence for extreme puritans. The Scotch brought with them to Canada "that nameless haunting guilt they never understood"; being Scotch "seems like a kind of doom." In "Help Thou Mine Unbelief," MacLennan considers the current state of Christianity in contemporary culture, and seeks an explanation as to why many people, especially intellectuals, are now looking for ultimate meaning outside the Church. He says that it is only natural to feel indignation at "self-righteous puritans who would make little children feel guilty for their human nature, while at the same time withholding from them the release of confession and absolution." The portrait of a self-righteous puritan making a little child feel guilty will suggest, to anyone who has read *Each Man's Son*, the scene where Mrs. MacCuish teaches the terrified Alan to say, "I am a miserable sinner and I know I will be damned." MacLennan claims that, rather than blaming the Protestant clergy, it would be far more sensible "to forget this futile, haunting primitive sense of guilt which is the worst legacy of puritanism – while we try in all humility to understand what is happening to our spiritual lives."

MacLennan's article, "The Defence of Lady Chatterley," sheds considerable light on his antagonism to the puritan denunciation of sex. MacLennan mounts a spirited defence of Lawrence's affirmation of the proper place for sex in man's life, and terms this affirmation *moral*. We feel that MacLennan is emotionally involved in the subject. This involvement will become clear as we proceed, for MacLennan's novels indicate that his own attitude is close to Lawrence's. MacLennan believes that the puritan conception of sex as evil is a perversion of the teachings of Jesus. Defending Lawrence, MacLennan suggests that a partial explanation for this puritan perversion may be found in the violent times in which St. Augustine and other early Church Fathers lived. Since the Romans of the decline were decadent in their use of sex, Augustine would hardly be able to avoid thinking of sex as one of the chief evils of his society, and one of the main reasons for its decline. Small wonder, then, that this forceful genius should have been able to give to his personal hatred and fear of sex the force of a primitive taboo. (Augustine's idea is parodied amusingly in *Two Solitudes,* in the portrait of the ideal wife and mother admired by the Methuens: plain, sexless, not the kind of woman who has caused the "ruination" of the Babylonians, Greeks, Romans, etc.)

St. Augustine's basic attitude towards sex as evil was later reinforced by Calvinism, and is still operative today. The "infantile" sexual attitudes of modern man are thus explained by MacLennan as a misinterpretation of Jesus' teaching, a mistake of St. Augustine and other Church Fathers, which was later reinforced by Calvin and Knox. MacLennan claims that Augustine followed Paul in holding that life is evil because man is a fallen creature: "If life is evil, then the sexual act must be the most evil act a human being can commit because it perpetuates life. What Augustine elevated into a cornerstone of Christian ethics, Calvin and Knox many centuries later translated into the everyday lives and institutions of their puritan followers."⁵ Thus MacLennan blames these "dark minds" for distorting the teachings and personality of Jesus. He sees the genius of Lawrence as being pitted against the old "taboo-morality" of Augustine and Calvin. (This is, of course, an oversimplification and, many theologians would argue, a falsification of Calvin's ideas. But we are, for the moment, primarily concerned with the attitudes of MacLennan.)

The puritan compulsion to work, which MacLennan has associated in his essays with mass production and materialism, is closely connected with the puritan suspicion of beauty and pleasure. In "Cross Country," MacLennan says that both Canadian and American puritans consider usefulness a higher virtue than beauty. In "The Art of City Living," he quotes with approval Francis Bacon's remark that crafty men condemn studies, simple men admire them, and wise men use them, and applies it to the North American continent under puritan influence. He says the puritans were neither crafty nor wise, but that only the gullible would dismiss them as simple: "Not the least of the scurvy tricks they played on humanity was the limitation they placed on that fine word useful. Anything not immediately applicable to the production, distribution and acquisition of material goods they considered to be of no use whatever." Music, painting and literature did not fit into the puritan's simplistic philosophy nor into his narrow definition of utility. MacLennan, let us note, is not objecting to the standard of utility but only to a certain interpretation of what constitutes it.

In connection with this disregard for beauty and the arts, it is interesting to note the view of puritanism advanced by E. K. Brown in the early forties, in his analysis of Canadian literature's distinguishing characteristics up until that time. The definition of puritanism which is implicit in the following remarks is obviously similar to MacLennan's use of the term:

> If Puritanism operated simply to restrain the arts within the bonds of moral orthodoxy, its effects, though regrettable, would be much less grave than they now are. Puritanism goes beyond the demand for severe morality: it disbelieves in the importance of art. . . . To popularize orthodox morality and to provide light, clean fun – that is the very limit of what the arts can be allowed to do without alarming the Puritan mind. For the Puritan a life devoted to one of the arts is a life misused: the aesthetic life is not a form of the good life.[6]

The pleasures of the palate are even less acceptable. In "By Their Foods . . . ," MacLennan refers to the puritan idea that pleasure in food is a sin. He lays the blame for tasteless and carelessly prepared Canadian food on the puritan tradition. The puritans would not be upset by this charge, interpreting "tasteless" to mean wholesome, and "carelessly prepared" as an indication that "we are a people with no nonsense about us, reserving our full energies for things higher than sensual pleasures, of which the pleasures of the table are unquestionably the lowest." (*RS* 20)

In "The Lost Love of Tommy Waterfield," MacLennan tells of a schoolboy friend with a God-fearing aunt who always drew the blinds on Sundays so that Tommy couldn't watch the boats breaking the gloom of the Lord's Day by sailing on the North West Arm. This last anecdote recalls Macauley's gibe: "The Puritans hated bearbaiting not because it gave pain to the bear but because it gave pleasure to the spectators." Macauley and MacLennan would seem to have similar conceptions of the term.

We have seen that in his use of the word "puritanism," MacLennan is consistent. He uses it with entirely negative associations which might be summed up in his phrase, "an ancient curse." We have noted the one exception to this usage in the essay which referred to the strengths and weaknesses of the puritans. Puritanism, then, by MacLennan's definition, is a spectre at the feast of life – a spectre which he is determined to exorcize.

MacLennan is consistent in his essays, which deal with ideas in a relatively abstract and logical way. Complications arise when we look closely at his novels. Here, amid the complexity of existential situations, some of the responses which he has denounced as puritan are seen to have an intimate connection with the values he wishes to affirm. Beauty, for example, is never considered evil or undesirable by MacLennan. It is, however, sometimes seen as *inferior good* which must be sacrificed in the interests of moral duty or the welfare of others. Similarly, situations arise where the restraint of emotions is seen as admirable in itself or necessary for the good of others. Like D.H. Lawrence, MacLennan sees man's sexual nature in a moral frame of reference. Sexual desires cannot be indulged indiscriminately. And finally, although the compulsion to work is condemned by MacLennan as neurotic, his novels on the whole constitute a defence of the value and necessity of work, in order that man may fulfil his own nature, and reform and improve society.

In recent years, many Canadians have discovered in themselves the same ambivalence which underlies MacLennan's fiction. He has accused religion of having enormously inhibited the Canadian character, yet he has declined to acknowledge, in connection with his attacks on puritanism, the part played by this religious tradition in his own artistic vision. MacLennan's values are often based in self-denial, so that the two conceptions of puritanism are seen to be related to one another, and certain aspects of the puritanism which he is attacking are involved in the ideals being affirmed in his novels. MacLennan's fiction is basically ambivalent with respect to action, work and enjoyment. In our eagerness to rid ourselves of what MacLennan calls an old "taboo-morality," we Canadians have found ourselves in similar dilemmas, struggling to recover values which have been twisted out of shape, sometimes altered beyond recognition, by extreme forms of puritanism.

NOTES

1. Cf. "Because Judaism is a religion which requires knowledge – we believe that only the knowledgeable can be pious." Rabbi Aaron Nussbaum, in "Families pay high price to buy Jewish education for 9,200 children in Toronto," *The Globe and Mail*, March 25, 1971, p. W7.

2. Norah Story, *The Oxford Companion to Canadian History and Literature* (Toronto: Oxford University Press, 1967), p. 387.

3. Perry Miller and T.H. Johnson, *The Puritans: A Sourcebook of Their Writings* (New York: Harper & Row, 1965), I, 1.

4. The depiction of American behaviour and attitudes in "Tora Tora Tora," the 1970 documentary film about the Japanese attack on Pearl Harbour in 1941, suggests that puritan self-discipline and devotion to work and duty were perhaps less strongly entrenched in the American character by 1941 than MacLennan would have us believe.

5. Hugh MacLennan, "The Defence of Lady Chatterly," *Canadian Literature*, 6 (Autumn 1960), 22.

6. E.K. Brown, *On Canadian Poetry* (Toronto: Ryerson, 1943), in *Masks of Fiction*, ed. A.J.M. Smith, NCL 02 (Toronto: McClelland and Stewart, 1961), p. 50.

2 FROM PRIMNESS TO SEXACOLA IN ONE GENERATION

Ottawa: "This prim little capital that could be so terrible. . . . This dull little place that had withered so many hearts. This little capital that had grown out of a lumber town with the enormous land spreading away from it from coast to coast and all the way up to the North Pole." (*RS* 83) It's all there as MacLennan sees it: the prim puritan past, and the mystic potential of a people and a land too vast, as he says on the last page of the same novel, even for fools to ruin all of it.

MacLennan, novelist and essayist, is a professor of literature at McGill University. Cohen, poet and novelist, is today best known to many as a singer of folk-rock ballads. What does their fiction have in common? Contrary to first impressions, there are profound similarities in the thematic concerns and underlying attitudes. Both of these Canadian writers are in the tradition of that puritan archmoralist, D.H. Lawrence, although the popular image of MacLennan and Cohen could hardly be more dissimilar.

Cohen's two novels are both products of the sixties. MacLennan's sixth novel, *Return of the Sphinx* (1967) was published just after Cohen's second, *Beautiful Losers* (1966). MacLennan was viewed as an iconoclast in Canada in the forties and early fifties. His novels and essays have played a part in helping to change the general cultural climate. Thus Cohen's freedom to publish novels in which sex is presented in a way that would never have been countenanced in Canada ten years earlier may be traced (at least in some small measure, for there is a complex web of cultural forces at work here) to MacLennan's writing. And Cohen's iconoclastic attitudes towards sex are indicative of changes in Canadian society, rather than being simply an individual phenomenon.

In a talk originally given on the CBC "Anthology" programme, MacLennan submitted that "our basic attitudes to society have changed inwardly out of recognition since the war."[1] Certainly we all know that topics are discussed openly today which would never have been aired in public only a short time ago. Robert Fulford and Arnold Edinborough, who were among Canadian writers gathered in 1967 to discuss Canadian publishing, stressed that books had been published in Canada in the sixties which it would have been impossible to have published here in the fifties. Both Fulford and Edinborough gave as an example Cohen's novel, *Beautiful Losers.*[2]

Ten years later, in an address at Carleton University in Ottawa, in December 1969, MacLennan again stressed the changes in Canadian society over the past thirty years. He said that, when he began writing, Canadian ideals and values were largely those of Victorian or nineteenth-century England. By this he meant that the standards of conduct were based upon Christian ethics, with a puritan interpretation of what this involved. These standards had been under attack for several decades by European writers, but were still dominant in Canada at the beginning of World War II.

MacLennan proceeded to give various examples of actual Canadian reactions to the treatment of sex in Canadian literature. In the forties, Gwethalyn Graham's fine novel, *Earth and High Heaven*, about the proposed intermarriage of a Christian and a Jew, was criticized for its "unnecessary mention of sex." A Morley Callaghan book was banned from the city of Toronto. MacLennan's *Barometer Rising* was banned by the province of Manitoba as late as 1961, and the author received letters denouncing him for his heroine having a child outside marriage. In the late 1950's, the word "divorce" was still cut out of movies by the censor in Quebec. Anyone reading these novels today would be likely to consider them extremely conservative in their treatment of sex. Yet Canadian society was reacting to them with shock and outrage only a few years ago.

In November of 1960, Penguin Books were brought to trial in England by the Director of Public Prosecutions under the new Obscene Publications Act for their forthcoming edition of Lawrence's *Lady Chatterley's Lover.* Did the novel tend to "deprave and corrupt" those into whose hands it might fall? The immense weight of evidence given by writers, critics and teachers as to the novel's literary excellence and moral purpose staggered the prosecution. The final verdict: not guilty. On this continent, a United States Federal Court had decided the previous year that *Lady Chatterley's Lover* was not an obscene book. Canadian publishers had offered, through their association, to assist financially in this fight. We may now see these historic trials and the acquittal of Lawrence's novel as prophetic of the coming decade – prophetic at least in the measure of freedom granted in this area by society to the artist. Hindsight also suggests that it was inevitable that this freedom should be exploited by those whose attitudes towards sex were completely different from those of Lawrence the moralist.

Lawrence was a controversial figure during his lifetime, as Cohen is sure to be. Witnesses for the Defence at the prosecution of Penguin Books quoted with approval the famous passage from *Lady Chatterley's Lover* where Lawrence's hero claims, "It's the one insane taboo left: sex as a natural and vital thing." They described Lawrence's novel as "highly virtuous and, if anything, puritanical,"[3] and Lawrence's attitude towards sexual relations as reverential, even sacramental, based on the tenderness, compassion and sensitivity which makes sex human. They pointed to the difference between such attitudes and the degrading influence of contemporary films, television and advertising. The themes of *Lady Chatterley's Lover* are also found in the novels of Cohen and MacLennan: the reverence for sex and the happiness to be found in tenderness, the mystic sympathy for nature and for all living things, and the attack on the mechanization of humanity.

We have noted, in our first chapter, MacLennan's own defence of *Lady Chatterley's Lover*. In 1963, MacLennan reviewed Sara Harris' *House of the 10,000 Pleasures*, a book which records the life history of a Japanese geisha. MacLennan's review of this book is relevant to our study of the values affirmed by his fiction, and the relation between these values and his Canadian society, because it reflects his profound admiration for Tsuya Giku, the geisha in question. There is no real equivalent in Western society for the Japanese geisha (the word means art-person), whose strict training in music, dance, conversation and other arts begins at the age of six or seven. Japanese tourist literature generally emphasizes the geisha's artistic talents while taking refuge in a discrete ambiguity. Perhaps that is because post-war Japan has become infected by the kind of puritanism which MacLennan deplores. I have space here only to indicate that neither Miss Harris nor MacLennan is ignorant of the geisha's basic sexual role.

Nevertheless, MacLennan sees that the core of the old geisha code of behaviour is discipline, moral duty and self-sacrifice. I say "old" because the geisha code has not survived the assault made upon Japanese ways by American cultural patterns since the war, and post-war changes in morals and manners have been even more rapid in Japan than in Canada. The "false values" (MacLennan's words) of Tsuya Giku's daughter, a post-war geisha, are shown in this book to be completely different from those of her mother, the woman whom MacLennan admires as "deeply moral," and whom he describes as one of the "greatest ladies" he has ever encountered in literature. MacLennan compares the geisha Tsuya Giku to "a mother-superior whose experience has taught her much more about life than she will permit herself to utter," and her arduous and disciplined training to that of the strictest of convents. He quotes approvingly the author's introduction, praising the geisha's self-sacrificing spirit. MacLennan concludes: "In brief, the geisha is as dedicated to men, to the preservation of their well-being, their mental balance and their competence as leaders, as the sisters of a religious order are dedicated to their god."[4]

In this review, MacLennan contrasts Japanese society, "which always had regarded physical love-making as the supreme experience, not casually to be acquired, and as subtle and difficult to master in its infinite shades of variation as the ballet," with what he calls "the Judaeo-Christian consciousness of sexual guilt." It is not difficult to see which society has his approval. It is also significant that MacLennan seems more interested in the geisha's *attitudes* of moral seriousness, dedication and discipline than in the fact that the *object* of her dedication is not God but the madam (a substitute parent) who has bought her in childhood, and the men whom she serves. The earnest morality of both Tsuya Giku and MacLennan exemplify what I will call, in my next chapter, the "mind" or characteristic attitudes of the historic Puritan.

The dust jacket of *Beautiful Losers* describes the novel as "a love story, a psalm, a Black Mass, a monument, a satire, a prayer, a shriek, a road map through the wilderness, a joke, a tasteless affront, an hallucination, a bore, an irrelevant display of diseased virtuosity, a Jesuitical tract, an Orange sneer, a scatological Lutheran extravagance – in short a disagreeable religious epic of incomparable beauty." Doubtless there are those who are able to see *only* the tasteless affront, the diseased virtuosity, the scatology; those who, as the Defence suggested in the trial of Penguin Books, are unable to see beauty and integrity where it exists. Subsequent readings may facilitate a saner view, as may the passage of time. Jacob Epstein's statues were tarred and feathered, and now they are in cathedrals.

When Cohen's novel was first published in 1966, H.R. Percy welcomed it "if only as a demonstration that literary censorship in

Canada is completely dormant. I had almost said dead, but the Grundy spirit is never that."[5] Percy noted that much of the adverse criticism was tepid rather than hostile, and that critics deplored rather than condemned, while acknowledging the "redeeming flights" of lyricism.[6] Certainly the latter is a superficial view. When form and content in *Beautiful Losers* are considered in relation to one another and to the whole novel, it must be evident to even the most bigoted that Cohen's indelicacy is not an end in itself.

Michael Ondaatje writes: "When *Beautiful Losers* was published in 1966 the critics went at it with whips. One reviewer said he saw nothing beautiful in it, just dirt and death. Safer critics tended to sit on a fence and say there was brilliant writing but was Leonard Cohen putting us on or not?"[7] Ondaatje's own opinion, that the novel is the most vivid, fascinating and brave modern novel he has read, grew from second thoughts about the book. I will confess, with Ondaatje, that a second reading was necessary before I appreciated this novel. On first reading, certain scenes came across well, but I was somewhat stunned by the no-holds-barred descriptions of sex. For a Canadian puritan, this book can be shock treatment. Culture shock. Reading it again several years later, I saw the strong thematic unity, the superb technical control over the point of view, the side-splitting comedy in what had shocked me first, and the reverential mystique of the holiness of the body and the entire natural world.

In 1943, E.K. Brown described "our strong Puritanism" as one of the limiting factors in Canadian literature. He claimed that foreign observers noted with amazement the avoidance of themes or language that might irk the puritan, and that Canada had, to that date, never produced works of literature offensive to puritan sensibilities or counter to the prevailing moral and social standards. By the early 1940's, he observed a slight crack in the dyke: "Even our Canadian Puritanism, however, has not been proof against the international currents of moral relaxation which have coursed so strongly during the past quarter century. In the poetry of those who are now approaching their fortieth year, there is a broad range of emotion, which does not stop short of carnality. . . ."[8] Brown believed that the mind of the good citizen of 1943 would boggle at a Canadian Whitman or Dos Passos. Perhaps his own mind would have boggled, at that date, at *Beautiful Losers*.

Conservative Canadians may view the social changes in this country in the last two decades as being summed up in the words of a 1971 newspaper headline: MORALITY STRONGHOLD YIELDS TO PORNOGRAPHY. The article in question dealt with

Texas, long a stronghold of conservative and traditional morality, and now a centre (with California and New York) for explicit commercial sex in theatres and newsstands. Staged sexuality, in productions such as "Oh! Calcutta!," "Che" and "Hair," is a relatively new phenomenon and is certainly not confined to Texas. It would have been difficult to convince a pre-war Canadian that a spectacle like "Hair" would run for some weeks and be well attended in Toronto and Ottawa in 1970–1.[9]

The entire Western world is caught up in these changing attitudes. A London gynecologist told an international medical congress meeting in April 1971 that "the kiss of the 1940's and 1950's has now become the sexual intercourse of the 60's and 70's."[10] Dr. J. Slome was giving a paper on abortion and the unmarried mother. Many of the patients who came under his care had told him that their pregnancies had resulted from casual friendships, and he noted that these patients illustrated the changing patterns of social behaviour during the last twenty years.

We live in a brave new world of sexuality. It seems that we are adopting as our own the old Neapolitan proverb which describes sex as the poor man's opera. Canadians, possibly because of the puritan tastes of their ancestors, have never been great opera fans. But the popularity of the poor man's version seems to be reaching a new high. There is no social science that accurately measures changes in social behaviour with regard to sex, although a number of sociologists and anthropologists are now studying this area. Sexual research developed from pioneers such as Krafft-Ebing, Freud and Marie Stopes, to the Kinsey studies of 1948 and 1953, and the Masters-Johnson publications of 1966 and 1970. Whereas the pioneers in this field were often vilified, today's researcher is likely to make a fortune publishing a report of his investigations. But it is difficult to determine whether we are really moving towards a new sexual consciousness, as writers like N.O. Brown and Herbert Marcuse suggest, or simply creating new myths no better than the old.

One of the most startling examples of the new sexual permissiveness is group sex amongst married couples. The participants call themselves "swingers." One anthropologist has estimated that by late 1970 between one and two million people were involved in the United States. Stewart Kent, who edits *Aware*, a monthly Canadian magazine devoted to bringing together and enlightening the swingers of Canada, estimates that there are 6,000 couples in this country who swing on a regular basis. The spousal and familial *togetherness* emphasized by women's magazines in the late 1950's has been taken a step further than the framers of the slogan intended. William French, in his review of Gilbert Bartell's *Group Sex*, describes the swingers as follows: "They view their institutionalized promiscuity as their entry into the jet set, the world of Beautiful People. The irony is that in all other respects they're very square – anti-hippie, racist, reactionary in politics (40 per cent. said they admired George Wallace). . . . Their only other hobby is watching television. Yet, in their confused scale of values, they believed their act of rebellion against sexual conventions made them liberal freethinkers."[11]

Marriage counsellors see in this behaviour a fear of getting close to one person, the attempt to maintain psychological distance by diffused sexuality. Group sex means depersonalized sex, since one of the unwritten rules is that one couple never exchange with another couple more than once (in order to avoid emotional involvement). The tom-cat syndrome. Thus group sex avoids intimacy in the very act of seeming to seek it. A sociologist at the University of Toronto notes the clash between group sex and traditional Canadian morality: "After all, this is basically a religious country with fairly strong beliefs in right and wrong conduct backed up by faith in a Christian God."[12] He fears that those participating in group sex will probably be subject to serious psychological problems.

It is interesting to compare a recent Ontario obscenity trial with the history-making trials on two continents of Lawrence's *Lady Chatterley's Lover*. In March 1971, the Ontario Court of Appeal dismissed an appeal by Ivan Reitman and Daniel Goldberg from their earlier conviction for producing an obscene movie, "The Columbus of Sex." The ninety-five minute film had been made at McMaster University with university students and faculty wives playing the roles, and had been shown there to students and faculty in August 1969. It was the first film to be tried in Canada under the obscenity law. After the film had been banned in this country under the Criminal Code, it was sold to Hollywood to become the basis of a "new" movie, "My Secret Life." Lawyer John Bowlby, appealing the conviction of Reitman and Goldberg, made the curious suggestion that university campuses are "unique isolated communities" which should be exempt from the laws applicable to the rest of society. (Many university students, on the contrary, are currently in favour of increasing the university's relevance to and integration with the rest of society.)

It is obvious that very few Canadians have seen, or been permitted to see, "The Columbus of Sex." Many of us, however, will have read the defence of this film written by its Canadian director John Hofsess and published in *Saturday Night*, August 1970. His arguments there are confused and contradictory. He alternates between insisting, on the one hand, on the film's *artistic* merit ("It was intended only for restricted distribution on the university circuit of film societies, and occasional showings in art centres"; "art to me is one of the few remaining areas of modern life where truth may be told . . . an authentic work of art has a cleansing and healing effect") and, on the other, on its *moral* purpose: "As in My Secret Life, the emphasis of Columbus of Sex is on its honesty, *not matters of aesthetics;* on moral ideas, *not artistic conventions* [italics mine]." In the main, Hofsess' arguments echo those advanced for the defence of *Lady Chatterley's Lover*, and Hofsess would have us believe that his film is a serious contribution to the moral edification of the nation – a puritan tract, as it were. He speaks of the therapeutic effects of exorcizing guilt feelings, of raising the moral tone of the nation: "It was the aim of Columbus of Sex to offer a redemptive vision of human sexuality."

He doth protest too much. Hofsess' own article, as much as the various newspaper accounts of the affair, leaves one totally unconvinced that the film is either artistic or moral. But the controversy raises some interesting matters for speculation. Surely the mistake of the official censors, in the past, has been to foster the hatred and suspicion of *the body as evil*. This is a form of the Manichaean heresy which has dogged Western society for nearly 2,000 years. The novels of D.H. Lawrence, Leonard Cohen and Hugh MacLennan (with the possible exception of the ending of *The Watch That Ends the Night*) are set firmly against this lie. But the pornographer's lie, if we may call it that, is to try to equate the Lawrencian acceptance of the body and its natural acts with the exploitation of the body (including lust and cruelty) for commercial profit; to pretend, in effect, that *all* expressions of sexuality are, or deserve to be, on a par with the tender interpersonal relationships affirmed by Lawrence's fiction. This attempted equation is patently false. The pornographic exploitation of the body is simply the Manichaean contempt in a different guise.[13]

Sexploitation films. Topless waitresses. Easy divorce. Open Sunday. Bikinis, mini-skirts, hot pants, and body-conscious knits. Canadian puritans have come a long way. Robert Fulford, speaking at an obscenity trial concerning the cover of the underground newspaper *Harbinger*, defended the surrealist drawing of a woman giving birth. He described it as an attempt to express the close relationship between good and evil, and said: "The Canadian public is tolerant of frank visual expressions."[14]

Where are we going? Many are confused, torn between old and new attitudes, as to what constitutes moral behaviour. There are already signs of a conservative backlash in the film industry in the United States. Sexploitation movie houses in Los Angeles suffered badly at the box office in 1970, and many skinflick theatres there reverted to showing legitimate movies. Unrestricted pornography leads to boredom and the law of diminishing returns. One Scandinavian scientist referred to the banana boat effect: "When bananas first appeared in Copenhagen after the war everyone ate themselves sick."[15] The coming trend is sweetness and light, as indicated by the popularity of Erich Segal's *Love Story*. Teenagers are back to romance and consider a phenomenon like group sex a "freak scene." (Out of the mouths of babes. . . .)

Perhaps the seventies will see many of those who have been down the permissive road a piece turning back to join hands with the conservative moralists who never set foot on it. These include members of Canadian organizations such as the Women's Christian Temperance Union, the Mass Media Bureau (a Roman Catholic group concerned with the moral quality of movies), and the Teen Challenge Narcotherapy Centre in Richmond B.C., where youths are trying to quit their drug habits by turning to religion. Members of such organizations try to brake or reverse trends towards permissiveness. The social and political power of such groups, as Alan Walker notes, was much higher some years ago than it is today.[16]

There are still those (especially in rural and small-town areas) who have never budged from the attitudes which were common in Canada prior to World War II. In the fall of 1971, a grade nine home economics teacher in a small town in Saskatchewan was fired for allowing her students to read her personal copy of the Vancouver underground newspaper *Georgia Straight*. The school board considered the references in the paper to sex unsuitable for "children" aged fourteen to sixteen.[17]

Writing in 1967 of the increasing evidence and importance of the ethnic population of Toronto, MacLennan welcomes the possibilities in these new cultural groups. Toronto is no longer the bastion of British dominance in Canada, and lovers of good cooking, good music and good theatre can rejoice. The ethnic groups, he implies, are non-puritan by his own definition of the term. MacLennan praises the New Canadians for their high level of education and their energy – standards which betray his own Puritan heritage. He describes the "great shift in Canadian morals and mores" which began after World War II as being even more obvious in Toronto than in Montreal: "The traditional puritanism has cracked wide open – with *mixed results.*"[18]

MacLennan does not mention, in what follows, what he believes to be the bad side of the coin in this development. But the reader of *Return of the Sphinx* may recall the author's obvious disdain for the sexy street-corner teenagers, and find these satirical descriptions relevant here. In a long newspaper article written shortly after the October Crisis of 1970, MacLennan contrasts what he calls the two totally different kinds of society depicted in his novels *Two Solitudes* and *Return of the Sphinx.*[19] He quotes approvingly the opinion of a middle-aged Montreal taxi-driver, to the effect that the youth of today have been spoiled and encouraged to believe that the world stood in awe of them.[20] He contrasts Marius Tallard, in *Two Solitudes*, with Daniel Ainslie. Daniel is a student at the University of Montreal, as Marius had been fifty years before: "but now the university is not run by clergy but swarms with social scientists, propaganda, some degree of luxury and throbs with the sexual revolution."[21]

MacLennan then quotes from *Return of the Sphinx* a passage which will interest anyone familiar with his attacks, in earlier novels and essays, upon puritan inhibitions with regard to sex. On a hot night in Montreal, Daniel is walking to see his girl friend:

In a puddle of light in front of one of the little stores was a cluster of boys and girls drinking pop and fondling one another. The boys wore jeans and T-shirts and the hair of most of them was long and shaggy. The girls were in hip-and-thigh stretchies of thin material and bright colours so that their lines were as clearly drawn as though they were naked. A girl giggled as Daniel walked past and the expressions on the faces of the boys made him think of calves. "Sexacola and Saturday night," he muttered to himself as he passed, and added the local slogan of the year, " '*Y a d'la joie!*' " . . . On this fantastically hot night the city was a bargain basement of raw sex on display, with thousands of females of all ages in those skin-tight garments that had come into fashion. . . . (*RS* 133–4)

The repulsion is Daniel's, and Daniel's sexual asceticism (puritanism, in MacLennan's terms) is generally deplored. But the context suggests that the repulsion felt for the giggling teenagers in their body-conscious clothing is also MacLennan's. The behaviour of the teenagers might appear to be a logical and inevitable development of the warfare against puritanism waged earlier only too successfully, so that MacLennan's position here suggests a retrenchment or conservative backlash. But the moral values affirmed in MacLennan's fiction over three decades are basically consistent. The change is simply one of emphasis. In the 1960's young people similar to those just described could be seen across the nation, and sex had become the favourite game of many North Americans. MacLennan is then forced to acknowledge an opposite danger, one which is as false (in his opinion) as the old enemy he calls puritanism. The dangers of over-permissiveness were ignored in his earlier writings because of the prevailing social attitudes.

Descriptions of the body-conscious teenagers recur in the novel, often contrasted with the black-robed figures of nuns: "The nuns were immediately followed by a trio of girls with slovenly hair and the lower halves of their bodies enclosed in skin-tight stretchies, one pink, one magenta, one yellow, and the buttocks of the one in magenta quivered like jello in a mold." (*RS* 18) Humour is an effective weapon here. Gabriel's war memories, merged with the death-dances of trillions of insects on a hot Montreal night, are succeeded by a description of "a thin-buttocked boy in jeans and a fat-buttocked girl in leotards" embracing one another frantically in a doorway. Beyond them, Gabriel sees the black outline of student priests. The description suggests that this kind of sex is neurotic, unhealthy. The frequent juxtaposition of the teenagers with nuns or priests points, without the necessity for further comment, to the contrast between the old Church-controlled mores and the new secularism. Writing in 1970, MacLennan emphasizes that the destructiveness of the revolutionaries is closely connected with the collapse of religion.[22] The revolutionaries he deplores. His attitude towards the passing of Church control is mixed, for he still opposes the attempt to control morality through guilt and fear. This is his old antagonist, the "ancient curse" depicted so vividly in *Each Man's Son*. In *Return of the Sphinx,* Daniel Ainslie has heard in a seminary a Jesuit sermon against fornication. When he first wakes after making love to Marielle he recalls the sermon and panics. The sermon is a classic of its type (Compare the one heard by Joyce's Stephen Daedalus in *A Portrait of the Artist as a Young Man*), and represents the same kind of emotional blackmail used in *Each Man's Son* by old Mrs. MacCuish upon the terrified child Alan.

"Death of a Victorian," the title of the book written by the protagonist in *Return of the Sphinx*, connotes the changes in attitudes and beliefs which have occurred in MacLennan's lifetime. And the Victorian who believes he has died is certainly MacLennan as well as his hero Ainslie.[23] "Victorian" stands for a whole complex of liberal optimistic beliefs, such as the belief that problems can be solved by education, and that man is basically good and steadily (if slowly) getting better. These were as common in Canada as in England until World War I, and were still common here until World War II. This continent did not experience the furies of two world wars fought upon its territory. The experiences of war on one's own soil is depicted by MacLennan as part of the Old World wisdom held by characters such as Gabriel Fleury and Marielle, who are "a war and a peace" *older* than young Canadians such as Chantal and Daniel Ainslie. Even Tarnley, whose business acumen is praised *ad nauseam* in the first book of *Return of the Sphinx* (in cliché descriptions of "appraising glances" shot from shrewd eyes), is the victim of this "Victorian" optimism. Alan Ainslie rejects as naïve Tarnley's hope for salvation through a select liberal arts college. And MacLennan has himself described as an exploded myth the idea that "the hope of civilization lies in universal education."[24]

I question, however, whether the Victorian in either Ainslie or his creator is entirely dead. Part of the Victorian credo, such as the activist reforming urge and the respect for the intellect, coincides with Puritan characteristics, although we cannot accuse the Puritan of Victorian *naïveté* with regard to the reality of evil. Daniel tells Marielle that his father was always happy to see him studying, overjoyed when he got good reports, and constantly speaking of the necessity for Canada to *earn* her way into civilization. And one of Ainslie's last appeals to his son (an appeal made long after the Victorian in Ainslie is supposed to have died) is "to learn some more," to go abroad to study as Ainslie had done.

Before turning to an examination of the novels of Hugh MacLennan and Leonard Cohen, I propose to discuss the basic attitudes and ideals of the English Puritans in the sixteenth and seventeenth centuries. It will be seen that there are many parallels between these historic Puritans and our two Canadian writers. Puritanism in our own century should be examined in relation to the historic context. When puritanism is placed in this wider frame of reference, MacLennan's negative definition will appear biased. His own phrase concerning the strengths and weaknesses of puritans is more accurate. Historic Puritanism, I shall argue, did indeed have strengths. MacLennan's own values will frequently prove to be very close to those of the historic Puritans.

NOTES

1. Hugh MacLennan, "The Story of a Novel," in *Masks of Fiction*, ed. A.J.M. Smith, NCL 02 (Toronto: McClelland and Stewart, 1961), p. 36.

2. See "Canadian Publishing," *Canadian Literature*, 33 (Summer 1967), pp. 7-8.

3. C.H. Rolph, ed., *The Trial of Lady Chatterley* (Penguin, 1961), p. 185.

4. Hugh MacLennan, "A Writer's Diary," *Ottawa Journal,* June 1, 1963.

5. H.R. Percy, "A Critic at Large," *Ottawa Journal,* June 11, 1966.

6. In an interview with Michael Harris, "Leonard Cohen: The Poet as Hero. 2," *Saturday Night,* June 1969, p. 29, Cohen said that he had never received a good review "up to the past year or two."

7. Michael Ondaatje, *Leonard Cohen*, Canadian Writers No. 5 (Toronto: McClelland and Stewart, 1970), p. 45.

8. E.K. Brown, *On Canadian Poetry* (Ryerson, 1943), reprinted in *Masks of Fiction* (1961), p. 50.

9. Cf. Ross Wetzsteon, "Staged Sexuality," in *The New Eroticism,* ed. Philip Nobile (New York: Random House, 1970): "don't we need to retain one final refuge, one final last act we will *always* refuse to simulate . . .?" (p. 185); "ultimately, then, I would argue that actors who perform sexual intercourse on stage are debasing themselves by performing a personally meaningful act for social and artistic goals, by performing an ultimate act for simulated purposes." (p. 186)

10. "Kissing just not enough for today's girl: doctor," *Globe and Mail*, April 2, 1971, p. 9.

11. William French, "Observing the Swinging Explosion," *Globe Magazine*, April 10, 1971, p. 15.

12. Jack Batten, "Marriage is one man one woman, one man one woman, one man . . .," *Globe Magazine*, June 5, 1971, p. 6.

13. See "Pornographic films: a $2 billion industry centred in San Francisco," *Globe and Mail*, March 13, 1971, p. 21. San Francisco also leads in alcoholism and suicides. The San Francisco vice-squad chief said that a well-known pornographic movie maker once told him that "anything that made women look like stupid meat, that degraded and hurt them, would make money." Art Mitchell, a pornie film king in San Francisco, told reporter Betty Lee that he was not worried about obscenity trials: "We've got a name psychiatrist to show that these films do not evoke an unhealthy or shameful response in people. We've even got a local film critic who swears they're downright educational."

14. "Harbinger cover not obscene, judge rules," *Globe and Mail,* May 18, 1971.

15. "Melancholy dealers say something's rotten in the state of porno," *Globe and Mail*, May 1, 1971.

16. See Alan Walker, "Can righteousness triumph over drink, drugs and dirty movies?" *Canadian Magazine*, February 27, 1971, p. 2: "Once upon a time, Canadians were cautious lovers, furtive drinkers – and they probably thought marijuana was a small town in Mexico. Today, sex, booze and pot float serenely along in the mainstream of the New Morality – to the joy of many worldly citizens, but to the despair of Canada's many moralist holdouts."

17. See "Saskatchewan teacher dismissed for displaying Georgia Straight," *Globe and Mail*, October 7, 1971.

18. Hugh MacLennan, *The Colour of Canada*, The Canadian Illustrated Library (Toronto: McClelland and Stewart, 1967), p. 71, italics mine.

19. See Hugh MacLennan, "Murder of truth . . . murder of people," *The Gazette*, Montreal, November 21, 1970, p. 7.

20. The cab-driver is quoted by MacLennan as follows: "How can they have fear, when nobody ever, their parents or their teachers, ever did anything but kiss their arses?" In *Return of the Sphinx,* police detective Lacombe has similar opinions.

21. *Ibid.*, p. 8.

22. *Ibid.*, p. 7.

23. Cf. Hugh MacLennan, "An Orange from Portugal," in *Modern Canadian Stories*, ed. G. Rimanelli and R. Ruberto (Toronto: Ryerson, 1969), p. 98: "We were simply a part of it [war], swept into it from the mid-Victorian Age in which we were all living until 1914."

24. Hugh MacLennan, "Murder of truth . . .," *Gazette*, November 21, 1970, p. 7: "If the Canadian crisis this fall did nothing else, it exploded before our eyes two great myths of the post-war world – that in the Electronic Village, the media link us with instant reality and that the hope of civilization lies in universal education."

3 THE PURITAN MIND IN THE SEVENTEENTH CENTURY

Historic Puritanism, in the England and New England of the seventeenth century, is by no means identical with MacLennan's negative definition of puritanism. While it does indeed contain the attitudes and tendencies which he attacks, it also represents ideals and values evidently cherished by MacLennan and affirmed by his novels. Certain aspects of historic Puritanism cast light upon MacLennan's attitude to puritanism today and help to explain an underlying ambivalence in his emotional approach, especially to the value of work. This discussion of historic Puritanism is only a context for my analysis of MacLennan and Cohen, as it is impossible in this space to do justice to the complexities of the subject.

In the seventeenth century the word already represented a wide spectrum of belief and practice. It was associated with parties of the Left, Right and Centre. Each of these contained within itself further differences and emphases, just as in contemporary political parties, and the problem is compounded by later meanings which attached themselves to the word. By the middle of the eighteenth century there had proceeded from Puritanism two radically opposed schools of thought: that represented by the evangelical religious sects on the one hand, and by the rationalists (Deists and forerunners of the Unitarians) on the other. Later groups stemming from the evangelicals or the rationalists may have retained something of the Puritan theology or of its intensity of spirit, but at the same time, according to Perry Miller, they threw aside so much of authentic Puritanism that the founding fathers would doubtless have repudiated such progeny.

Despite the wide range in sixteenth- and seventeenth-century beliefs, many writers on historic Puritanism suggest that there is a unity in the multiplicity. A general consensus in Puritan thought may be found in the philosophy of life and code of values to which the majority of Puritans subscribed. Miller speaks of a unity which can be seen in Puritan thought, expression and manners. A.S.P. Woodhouse, in his Introduction to the Army Debates from the Clarke Manuscripts, agrees with Miller that Puritanism is an entity, but he qualifies this statement with the reminder that the definition must be eclectic. He later adds the further qualification that it is unnecessary to posit a *unity* in all Puritan thought; it is sufficient to recognize a *continuity*. It is this unity or continuity which I seek to establish as a background for our Canadian heritage and for Mac-Lennan's thought. We are concerned, of course, not with the political aspects of historic Puritanism but rather with the religious, philosophic, social and intellectual characteristics of the seventeenth-century Puritan mind. I suggest that the unity or continuity of which Miller and Woodhouse speak is to be found in the Puritan attitude towards life – an attitude of moral seriousness, an overriding concern to discover (and do) man's duty towards God and his neighbour, and thereby to reform and improve society. A similar moral earnestness forms the background of MacLennan's own thought, as reflected in his novels.

Woodhouse suggests two definitions of Puritanism, both of which are used by historians, although the first is more common than the second:

It is possible to extend the term *Puritan* to cover all the varied forces generated by the Protestant Reformation. . . . Again it is possible to subdivide these forces and relegate the term *Puritan* to the more conservative, to those that remain strictly Calvinistic, adhering not only to the doctrine of predestination but also to the Genevan pattern in church and state, and opposing religious, while setting severe limits to political, liberty – or, in other words, to make *Puritan* practically synonymous with Presbyterian.[1]

The two definitions are not of course mutually exclusive. Each points, however, towards a different area of conduct and belief. My point is that MacLennan's definition of puritanism derives substantially from Woodhouse's second, or conservative, definition of Puritanism, and scarcely at all from the first.

Woodhouse suggests that the "holy community" is one of the ideals held, in some form, by all Puritan groups. Among the extremists the ideal assumes a menacing aspect, for the rule of the Saints is to be imposed by force. The ideals of the holy community were based upon the teachings of Protestant Christianity. The Puritan believed that God had spoken through his Word, the Christ, and that the written record of the historic revelation was contained in the Scriptures; he believed that these should be studied as a guide to daily life; and he tended to see secular life in theological terms. The Puritan, as Woodhouse notes, turned to the theological aspects of a question as naturally as the modern man turns to the economic. This response is peculiar to the Puritan in degree rather than in kind. The sacramental basis of Christianity witnesses to the belief in all nature having been penetrated by grace, the belief in God's immanence as well as transcendence. The Incarnation expresses this same unity. Yet in spite of the intimate relation which held, for the majority of Puritans, between religion and daily life, a dogmatic distinction between nature and grace led some Puritans to distinguish sharply between these two areas. This segregation tends to turn into a dualistic opposition of matter and spirit, and it encouraged some Puritans to reject the senses and the pleasures dependent upon them.

Eugene Osterhaven, writing of the Reformed tradition in our own time, acknowledges that for many Christians their consuming interest in the world to come militates against their appreciation of God's present creation: "There have been periods in the history of the church, particularly in times of persecution, when this position was adopted by many. Outstanding church leaders have been quoted in defence of this conception, Calvin among them."[2] Calvin's first chapter on "Meditation on the Future Life" refers to the necessity "to accustom ourselves to contempt for the present life." Osterhaven contends that selective quotation is unfair, and that interspersed throughout such negative judgements are equally strong statements of world acceptance and affirmation. In other sections dealing with the right use of this present life, Calvin writes that earthly life is never to be hated except in so far as it holds men subject to sin, and that not even hatred of this condition may properly be turned against life itself.

R.H. Tawney, in his study of the relation between religious ideas and economic movements in medieval and post-medieval Europe, emphasizes that religion was the prime influence on men's outlook on society in the sixteenth and seventeenth centuries. In *Religion and the Rise of Capitalism,* Tawney charts the economic interpretation of the Puritan's moral seriousness and his urge to reform society. MacLennan's social and economic ideals, implicit in his novels, can be understood better when we have understood the conflicting ideals of Calvin and Luther. MacLennan's own sympathies are with the Lutheran approach. Tawney describes Calvinism as a creed which sought not merely to purify the individual but to reconstruct

Church and State. Calvin based his social theory on economic ideas of a money economy – ideas which were relatively advanced for his time and are still operative today. Luther's economic ideas, on the other hand, were medieval, based on the traditional stratification of rural society and on a natural rather than a money economy. When the followers of Luther criticize economic abuses, "it is precisely against departures from that natural state of things – against the enterprise, the greed of gain, the restless competition, which disturb the stability of the existing order with clamorous appetites – that their criticism is directed."[3] Calvin broke with this medieval tradition to which Luther adhered, a tradition which regarded a preoccupation with economic interests beyond what is necessary for subsistence as reprehensible, which stigmatized the middle man as a parasite and the usurer as a thief. Tawney describes Luther as one who saw economic life with the eyes of a peasant and a mystic.

Hugh MacLennan is not a peasant but he is, at times, a mystic. MacLennan's entire attack on the New York advertising world, in *The Precipice*, has close affinities with the Lutheran approach to economics. This does not mean, of course, that he suggests a return to feudal conditions. It does mean that he thinks of honest, useful work as the proper economic basis for society, rather than the manipulation of capital and a pandering to the worst instincts of human nature through unprincipled advertising.

The satire against McQueen and Sir Rupert Irons in *Two Solitudes* stems from the same kind of thought. While MacLennan would certainly include intellectual and artistic labours within his definition of work (and here he differs from the puritanism he deplores) he refuses to include the efforts of McQueen, Sir Rupert and Carl Bratian. Those sympathetic to the idealism of the MacLennan-Lutheran position might call Calvin's economic ideas more cynical; others might call them more realistic. Calvin, and still more his later interpreters, did not regard with suspicion the mere fact of capitalistic enterprise in commerce and finance. They no longer stigmatized the businessman and the usurer whose profits, Calvin argued, came from his own diligence and industry. Of Calvinism Tawney writes:

It no longer suspects the whole world of economic motives as alien to the life of the spirit, or distrusts the capitalist as one who has necessarily grown rich on the misfortunes of his neighbour, or regards poverty as in itself meritorious, and it is perhaps the first systematic body of religious teaching which can be said to recognize the economic virtues. Its enemy is not the accumulation of riches, but their misuse for purposes of self-indulgence or ostentation. Its ideal is a society which seeks wealth with the sober gravity of men who are conscious at once of disciplining their own characters by patient labour and of devoting themselves to a service acceptable to God.[4]

This description of the Calvinist businessman is extraordinarily close to MacLennan's satirical portraits of Huntly McQueen and Sir Rupert Irons, archetypes of the Montreal Protestant businessman. The particular colouring which the Puritan reforming zeal takes in the Calvinist businessman is plainly antipathetic to Mac-Lennan, and he frequently presents this type as hypocritical. But his novels indicate that the reforming zeal itself, in other guises, is part of MacLennan's own approach to life.

It is a paradox that Calvinism, despite its repudiation of personal merit, is intensely practical. Good works are not a means but a proof of salvation, not a way of attaining God's grace but a sign that it has been attained. As for the moderate Puritan who was not disposed to prove his election or lack of it, the scriptural teaching of the fruit of the Spirit would be his authority for a continual striving after good works. Luther insisted that good works would be the fruit of salvation as vehemently as he denied that they could contribute to its attainment. It was thus that religious belief issued for the Puritan in a reforming zeal and an activist temperament. He must work to establish the Kingdom of God on earth. Woodhouse considers that the zeal for positive reform is one of the clearest marks of the Puritan, and that the Puritan temper is in general active rather than contemplative or mystical. Milton, for example, is the least mystical of the great religious poets. The practical and utilitarian character of Puritan witness, as loving *service* of God and man, is also emphasized by Eugene Osterhaven: "From the time of Calvin an emphasis upon practical Christian living has characterized the Reformed Church."[5]

This passionate zeal for reform may run counter to the ideal of liberty and toleration. Here the Puritans of the right may come close to the Roman Catholic ideas which were given institutional form in the Inquisition and the Index. Why should the liberty to do evil and to err, as the authorities understood these, be allowed? When the Puritan spoke of liberty, he meant Christian liberty: real freedom is the service of God. When he spoke of equality, it might be the limited equality of believers: "Liberty of conscience (falsely so-called) may in time improve itself into . . . liberty of perdition of souls and bodies."[6] An extreme interpretation and application of these ideas may be seen in the Massachusetts Bay theocracy, after its establishment in 1630. A concern for liberty and toleration, on the other hand, is manifested, by no means equally, among the different groups of the Puritan Left in England. The ideal of tolerance remains in uneasy alliance with the ideal of reform in the interests of righteousness. In the extreme intolerance of the Puritan Right, we see one of the characteristics of the puritanism which MacLennan is attacking.

We have been considering the moral seriousness of Puritanism, its urge to reform the world, and its tendency to see daily life primarily in moral terms. The Calvinist glorification of the financier and businessman represents one aspect of this moral seriousness which MacLennan finds unacceptable. In Calvinist theology we find the explanation for another aspect of the repressive puritanism which MacLennan is attacking. His antagonism to his Calvinist heritage can be clearly seen in his prefatory note to *Each Man's Son*, where the ancient curse which dogs the Scottish-Canadians is described as the belief that man is "sinful and doomed through no fault of his own," and exists "under the wrath of an arbitrary God who will forgive only a handful of His elect on the Day of Judgment." This antagonism is obviously related to the Calvinist doctrine of predestination, which places man's guilt and damnation outside the area of his own response to God's grace.

Predestination refers to God's eternal decree with respect to mankind's destiny. The Presbyterians, followers of Calvin and the party of the extreme right in seventeenth-century England, understood predestination as guaranteeing the absolute sovereignty of God and His grace. The Synod of Dort (1618–19) affirmed the view that from all eternity God wills that some should be pre-ordained to salvation and others passed over.[7] It defended the following five points: that God elects individuals to be saved; that he designs redemption for these elect only; that fallen man is of himself incapable of true faith and repentance; that God's grace is efficacious for the salvation of the elect; and that a soul once regenerated is never ultimately lost.

In later Calvinism, a further distinction was sometimes made. Some held that God both elects individuals to salvation and others to damnation (double predestination), while others believed simply in single predestination or election. Many of the Protestant Reformers embraced "double P" in principle. Writing in 1950, François Wendel takes issue with the majority of nineteenth- and early twentieth-century theologians, who saw predestination as the central doctrine of Calvin's theology. Wendel admits that Calvin attributed great importance to predestination in both its forms, election and reprobation. Wendel argues that "to recognize that Calvin taught double predestination and underlined its dogmatic and practical interest, is not to say that this must be taken to be the very centre of his teaching."[8] Wendel agrees with Paul Wernle, an early twentieth-century theologian, that faith in predestination is far from being the centre of Calvinism.

The layman will probably consider the argument as to whether predestination is central to the Reformed tradition or merely of "great importance" as splitting hairs. Indeed, anyone pursuing the controversy at length will begin to wonder how the Jesuits gained their superior reputation for casuistry (the query as to how many angels could dance on the head of a pin being commonly used as an example), when the honours might well belong to the Calvinists.

Contemporary neo-Reformed theologians such as Karl Barth and Emil Brunner maintain that the Augustinian and Calvinistic doctrines on predestination are unbiblical, and are corrupted by an abstract philosophical idea of God's omnipotence. This abstraction substitutes a mechanical principle of causality for the personal relationship between God and the human soul. Where the secular principle of causality posits necessity, the Bible posits a free and sovereign God who accomplishes, through His grace, whatsoever pleases Him.

The historic Puritans were by no means at one on the matter. The Arminians (followers of Jacob Arminius, a late sixteenth-century Dutch Reformed theologian) stressed the ability of man to respond to divine grace, and denied that He elects some men to be damned. (The bone on which MacLennan chokes is the concept of an arbitrary God, and of man condemned *through no fault of his own*, except the crime of being born as a man.[9]) The Synod of Dort was intended as a refutation of the Arminian doctrine known as The Remonstrance (1610). The Arminians asserted that God's decree establishes the principle that whoever believes on Jesus Christ will be saved, and that salvation is possible in principle for all men. In Puritan writings, the term Arminian came to be loosely used to designate the Laudian or Anglican position, especially with reference to the attitude on predestination, which was felt to be basic. The Arminian position stresses the personal quality of the human relation to the divine.

In 1630, William Prynne's *Anti-Arminianism* defended the extreme Calvinist position. In "seven dogmatical conclusions," Prynne maintains that God has predestined unto eternal life not all men but only a certain select number called the Elect; that the only cause of election is God's free grace, not the good works or efforts of the persons elected; that there is not any such thing as free will whereby men may repent and be saved by their own efforts; and that although Christ died "sufficiently" for all men, he died primarily and "effectually" for none but the Elect.[10] Prynne calls these assertions the established doctrine of the Church of England, but many Anglicans could not subscribe to them, as the Arminian dispute testifies. A belief in double predestination, and an obsession with guilt, are not central features of Protestant Christianity. This must be kept constantly in mind, as MacLennan tends to equate the former with Protestantism. These preoccupations, on the other hand, may represent one of the main strands of Protestant Christianity in the evolving culture of the British North American provinces, and this may help to account for the popular image of the word "puritan" today. Among the diverse groups of seventeenth-century English Puritans, the Calvinists represented the ultra-conservative position.

One more characteristic of historic Puritanism concerns us in relation to MacLennan. Puritanism emphasized man's reason. MacLennan also sets a high value on the intellect. His approach to writing in his novels as well as his essays, strikes one as being primarily a rational one, despite his own disclaimer.[11] The seventeenth-century Puritans were the heirs not only of medieval Christianity but also of the Renaissance. Milton's works represent a fusion of Puritanism with the Hellenistic spirit. Puritan sermons and pamphlets indicate that humanist culture tended to accentuate rationalism. John Cotton, writing in England in 1651, said that "knowledge is no knowledge, without zeale," but "zeale is but a wild-fire without knowledge."[12] Scholars living in the early seventeenth century still held to the medieval synthesis, still believed that all knowledge was one and was organized hierarchically to the glory of God. The leaders of the Puritan movement were men of learning. Although their religion rested upon faith, they demanded that it should be given a logical exposition.

At the same time, Puritanism was forever giving rise to rebellions against its own ideal of learned religion. The possibilities of a fanatical anti-intellectualism were latent in Luther's ideas of the soul's direct relation to God and of the priesthood of every believer. Luther himself would have been horrified to see his ideas pushed to this extreme, and the development did not come for more than a century after his time. In the seventeenth century the Protestants were struggling to maintain a complete harmony of reason and faith, science and religion. The seventeenth-century preacher made very little allowance for ignorance and stupidity in his audience. Perry Miller notes that all available evidence points to the fact that during the Puritan age in New England the common man was amazingly versed in systematic divinity: "A gathering of yeoman and 'hired help' around the kitchen fire of an evening produced long and unbelievably technical discussions of predestination, infant damnation, and the distinctions between faith and works."

It is a paradox that a dogma based ultimately on faith should foster a rational and intellectual spirit, but paradoxes are frequent in Christianity and in historic Puritanism. The revelation embodied in the Bible was held to be complete and unalterable, yet still subject to *progressive* comprehension and interpretation. Milton's *Areopagitica* emphasizes the place of free discussion in the understanding of revealed truth. Woodhouse considers this passionate search for truth, whether adequately or inadequately conceived, to be one of the lasting contributions of Puritanism. And it was accompanied by a confidence in truth's power to guard itself and to prevail if given an open field. Samuel Morison and Eugene Osterhaven join Miller and Woodhouse in emphasizing the intellectual element in historic Puritanism. Morison calls the Puritan creed "an intellectualized form of Christianity," which stimulated mental activity on the part of those who professed it.[13] Osterhaven concurs, noting that Calvin assured his listeners that Scripture is intelligible and that it was their duty to read and ponder it. The Puritan knew that the body requires intellectual as well as other kinds of food, "so that the common man was encouraged, even required, to read, think, and learn."[14]

This strong intellectual emphasis, characteristic of historic Puritanism, is found throughout the novels of Hugh MacLennan. He too is concerned to give a reason for the faith that is his. As a classical scholar, MacLennan shares this humanist tradition with the seventeenth-century Puritan. The humanist tradition of the Puritan scholars encouraged individualism as well as rationalism, and this too is one of MacLennan's ideals. The Puritan, encouraged by Luther, asserted the right and duty of thinking for himself. His guides were the Bible and his own conscience. Tawney calls this monasticism secularized. Luther argued that if man would observe the Golden Rule, and love his neighbours as himself, no law books or courts would be required.

MacLennan and Cohen share Luther's idealism and, at times, his lack of realism. Cohen sees the artist as the conscience of his race. Although his hero Breavman seems to set himself in opposition to his parents' code of behaviour, he is described as having inherited or taken upon himself all of their moral and social concerns, and he is depicted as being more moral than the adult community. The historic Puritan, like the Old Testament prophet, moralized the numinous experience of God. With the true puritan, as Woodhouse emphasizes, religion remains the first concern.

If by "religion" we mean the concern for ultimate values, and the conception of man as an ethical and spiritual creature, MacLennan and Cohen must be considered as religious writers.[15] But perhaps the word "religion" should be kept to denote belief in a Supreme Being, and participation in an established religious tradition or community. Consider the following definition by Perry Miller: "Puritanism was not only a religious creed, it was a philosophy and a metaphysic; it was an organization of man's whole life, emotional and intellectual, to a degree which has not been sustained by any denomination stemming from it."[16] MacLennan has the Puritan intensity with regard to moral problems. He has retained the Puritan idealism and moral earnestness without the Christian dogma. This is the positive side of MacLennan's own Puritan heritage. In his concern to repudiate the negative side of the coin, he has refused to allow the word "puritan" to carry this positive meaning.

But there is more involved than a problem in semantics or an arbitrary assignment of meaning. The two concepts, MacLennan's puritanism and historic Puritanism, do actually coincide to a certain extent, as we shall see. In the areas where they fuse, MacLennan's loyalties are divided and his emotions frequently opposed. Many a Canadian in the post-war cultural revolution has found himself caught in similar dilemmas, torn between the recognition that pleasure is certainly not wrong in itself, and the conviction that hedonism is a false philosophy and an empty substitute for religion.

NOTES

1. A.S.P. Woodhouse, ed., *Puritanism and Liberty: From the Clarke Manuscripts* (London: Dent, 1938), p. 35.

2. M. Eugene Osterhaven, *The Spirit of the Reformed Tradition* (Grand Rapids, Michigan: Eerdmans, 1971), p. 127.

3. R.H. Tawney, *Religion and The Rise of Capitalism* (Penguin, 1964), p. 112.

4. Ibid., p. 114.

5. Osterhaven, *The Spirit of the Reformed Tradition*, p. 111.

6. Thomas Case, *Spiritual Whoredom Discovered in a Sermon before the House of Commons, 26 May 1647*, p. 34, in Woodhouse, *Puritanism and Liberty*, p. 51.

7. Norah Story notes that the Calvinist doctrine of predestination was represented by crucifixes in which the arms of Christ were only partly

spread. One such crucifix is in the Fort Beauséjour National Museum. The doctrine was opposed by the Jesuits and condemned in a papal bill in 1713. See *The Oxford Companion to Canadian History and Literature* (Toronto: Oxford, 1967), p. 387.

8. François Wendel, *Calvin. The Origins and Development of His Religious Thought*, trans. Philip Mairet (London: Collins, Fontana, 1969), p. 264.

9. In a letter to John Gray, 1951, MacLennan wrote: "My mortal quarrel with Calvinism was not that it denied realities but that it inculcated into children the idea that God was each man's personal enemy and that a man committed a sin merely by existing." MacLennan Papers, quoted in Alec Lucas, *Hugh MacLennan*, Canadian Writers 8 (Toronto: McClelland and Stewart, 1970), p. 54.

10. See William Prynne, *Anti-Arminianism*, in Woodhouse, *Puritanism and Liberty*, pp. 232-3. Cf. Eugene Osterhaven, letter of June 17, 1971, to the author: "I would agree that every man has freedom of will, that will is understood as the whole man in response, and that we distinguish between this natural freedom of will and 'free will' in the sense of ability to know God and do good. . . . Whereas we all have the 'freedom' to make decisions – that is part of the meaning of being human – having free will in the sense of being free from the bondage of sin is a gift of the Holy Spirit and belongs to the children of God, i.e., those whose natures have been changed through the operation of God's Spirit. This is the old Puritan position."

11. See Hugh MacLennan, "Murder of truth . . . murder of people," *The Gazette*, Montreal, November 21, 1970, p. 7: "Contrary to what some critics say, I never planned my novels to illustrate social theses or national dilemmas. . . . Most theories I made were made after the novels were written." See also MacLennan, "Two Solitudes that Meet and Greet in Hope and Hate," *Maclean's*, August 1971, p. 19: "What I have felt has all my life been more important than what I have thought, for I am no intellectual." George Woodcock maintains that MacLennan's novels are "unashamedly didactic." See "A Nation's Odyssey," *Masks of Fiction*, ed. A.J.M. Smith (Toronto: Ryerson, 1961), p. 129.

12. John Cotton, *Christ the Fountain of Life* (London, 1651), p. 145, in Perry Miller and T.H. Johnson, *The Puritans: A Sourcebook of Their Writings* (New York: Harper & Row, 1965), I, 22.

13. S. Morison, *The Puritan Pronaos* (New York, 1936), in *Puritanism in Early America*, ed. George M. Waller (Boston: Heath, 1965), p. 78.

14. Osterhaven, *The Spirit of the Reformed Tradition*, p. 78.

15. Cf. Alec Lucas, *Hugh MacLennan*, p. 57: "MacLennan is essentially a religious novelist." Of *Beautiful Losers*, Leonard Cohen has said: "I was writing a liturgy . . . a great mad confessional prayer. . . ." Quoted in Michael Ondaatje, *Leonard Cohen*, Canadian Writers 5 (Toronto: McClelland and Stewart, 1970), p. 44. D. J. Jones, in *Butterfly on Rock* (Toronto: University of Toronto Press, 1970), p. 78, describes *Beautiful Losers* as "fundamentally a spiritual book."

16. Miller, *The Puritans: A Sourcebook*, p. 4.

4 MACLENNAN'S EARLY NOVELS: LIFE AGAINST DEATH

In his study of the psychoanalytical meaning of history, Norman O. Brown describes Freud's theory of the dualism which underlies human conflicts, a dualism which Freud sees in terms of two basic instincts driving men towards life or death. This dualism is grounded in the very nature of life. Freud describes the instincts in terms of a "pleasure principle" and a "reality principle." The latter is the cause of repression, the pillar on which Freud's theory of psychoanalysis rests. Brown finds the source of Freud's pessimism in this hypothesis of an irreconcilable conflict between human instincts: between Eros or sexual love, seeking to preserve and enrich life, and the death instinct, seeking to return life to the peace of death. Brown is attempting to account for the forward movement in Freud's thought, since many of Freud's later ideas are not in agreement with his earlier ones, and go beyond Freud to an optimistic theory of human life and history. Brown posits a primal unity, differentiation through antagonism, and final harmony or "redemption" in the reunification of the instinctual opposites. He argues that death, properly understood, is not the enemy of life.[1]

In seeing these instincts as a dialectical unity rather than an antagonistic dualism, Brown's thesis is similar to the metaphysic which underlies the fiction of D.H. Lawrence. Lawrence's essay, "The Crown" (1915), uses an imaginative rather than a didactic technique to show the dynamic interrelationship of these opposites as necessary to one another. "The Lion and the Unicorn are fighting for the Crown." The two fight everlastingly, in a "divine discontent," for the Crown of Life: "And there is no rest, no cessation of the conflict. For we are two opposites which exist by virtue of our inter-opposition."[2] And what does Lawrence intend by his two mythical beasts from the old nursery rhyme? Darkness and light, flesh and spirit, power and love, activity and passivity – as in the yin and yang of Taoist thought, the list is endless.

I suggest that Lawrence's attitude is very close to Brown's, whereas MacLennan's is similar to Freud's as here defined by Brown: namely, it posits a duality to be fought out rather than a dialectic between two very different but equally necessary forces. MacLennan, like Lawrence, is a moralist. Both men regard the body and sex, given certain conditions, as *good*. But MacLennan's metaphysic differs from that of Lawrence and Brown with regard to the desirability of the instincts which are not loving and peaceful, or life-seeking, in MacLennan's terms. His Puritan heritage would incline him to see the forces of life and death as forces for good and evil, irreconcilable opposites. MacLennan has interpreted his Calvinist heritage as basically life-denying, since in his experience the conviction of sin was necessarily accompanied by fear and guilt. Thus it became, for MacLennan, a death force. The patterns of imagery in his fiction and the alignment of his characters (as sympathetic and admirable, or the opposite) all centre in this contrast of life and death. And puritanism, as MacLennan defines it, is placed on the side of death.

MacLennan's early novels, *Barometer Rising*, *Two Solitudes* and *The Precipice*, will appear at first sight to constitute a consistent attack upon puritanism. In *Barometer Rising*, these attacks are casual rather than thematic. The consistency here is in MacLennan's underlying attitude, not in the frequency of his attacks. The social environment which forms the background for the major portions of these novels – the city of Halifax, the Protestant community of Montreal, the Roman Catholic parish of Saint-Marc-des-Érables, and the Ontario town of Grenville – is depicted in each case as uncompromisingly puritan. Various anecdotes and references widen the picture to include all of Canada and much of the United States. "God help us," exclaims Dennis Morey in *Two Solitudes*, "why do people hate beauty in this country the way they do?" He claims that puritan attitudes have ruined the city of Winnipeg. Similarly, Bruce Fraser says in *The Precipice* that until the Grenvilles of Canada are "debunked" from top to bottom, there will be no fun and no future for anyone in Canada.

Halifax provides the setting for *Barometer Rising*, and for one chapter in *The Precipice*, where the city is described as being dominated by Calvinists who think it more moral for a man to buy a bottle of whisky and drink it in secret in the park than to drink it comfortably in public. In *Barometer Rising*, the puritan environment of Halifax has necessitated Penny's three years of "secrecy and abnegation," years of bitterness during which she has been unable to enjoy beauty.

The Protestant community of Montreal is represented by the Methuen family and by a group of Presbyterian businessmen, especially Huntly McQueen and Sir Rupert Irons. McQueen's attitude towards work will be discussed in the next chapter. Our present concern is his attitude towards women, and towards pleasure in general. Although he admires Janet Methuen (the exact opposite of the sensuous Kathleen), he considers the prospect of marriage "embarrassing." The Methuen family distrusts physical beauty in women, who are "expected to be irreproachable wives and solid mothers of future Methuens, not females who might stimulate those pleasures the men of the family believed had caused the ruination of the Babylonians, Greeks, Romans, French . . . and various other minor races of the world." Dennis Morey, the officer who meets Kathleen Tallard in a Montreal hotel, describes his wife in terms similar to that of the Methuen ideal: irreproachable as a wife and mother, undeniably good, but totally lacking in imagination and humour.

One might suspect at this juncture that MacLennan does not admire goodness, but this soon proves to be an error. The Methuens admire art, but only when both art and artist are socially acceptable. Janet suspects the soldiers whom she serves in a war canteen of being immoral merely because of their rough language, and she and her Methuen in-laws appear to be totally incapable of appreciating the simple goodness of a man like Captain Yardley, her father, or the fine qualities of a young man like Paul Tallard. Both Paul and Heather, in their twenties, run away from Montreal to escape the strait-jacket of their background.

In the parish of Saint-Marc, the atmosphere is almost as puritan as it is in Grenville. Father Beaubien is described as having an eye for the length of the girls' dresses, and as seeing the devil every time a boy puts his arm around a girl when the moon is full. Father Beaubien maintains an atmosphere in the parish which Kathleen, Tallard's Irish wife, finds repressive. Preparing for dinner in Montreal with Dennis Morey, she dresses and makes up her face as she has not dared to do in Saint-Marc.

Marius Tallard, Athanase's son, both fears and despises sex. He is fascinated by the pictures of nude women in his father's art books: "They signified only the female being he did not know, the being which was beautiful and dangerous and at the core of sin." The sensual beauty which Kathleen embodies both repels and attracts him. He feels that she has made the atmosphere of the house "mysteriously evil, warm with sin." It is not just her beauty but its sensual quality which Marius fears. His puritan attitude has been inherited from his mother, whose memory he worships. Marie-Adèle, Athanase's first wife, had estranged herself from Athanase soon after their marriage and had sought to make a devotional piety her whole life. After her death, Athanase thinks that his first wife never lived for life, "but in order to die, in order to enter the Kingdom of Heaven."

In *The Precipice*, the town of Grenville makes itself felt as a personal character. Although there are five parts in the novel, the first, dealing with Grenville, occupies one half of the whole. It concentrates on the town's puritan attitudes, for the problems of the chief characters can only be understood against this background. Matt McCunn describes puritan towns such as Grenville as prematurely old, old, "like respectable women" before they ever start living. Lucy Cameron's Uncle Matt is a non-puritan individualist, of whom the townsfolk strongly disapprove. Talking with Matt in the Grenville drugstore, Lucy encounters Ike Blackman, the town's most disreputable character. Using Ike, Matt and the Greek waitress, MacLennan humorously sketches the town's disapproval of drink, sex and Ike's avoidance of "honest work." MacLennan depicts puritanism as working through social approval or disapproval to limit and restrict freedom. Lucy realizes that, in a town like Grenville, personal freedom will necessarily be accompanied by a bad reputation.

The negative and repressive influence of puritanism is represented in Part One by deathly images of blankness and freezing, of walls and rigid molds. Lucy feels the town to be closing in around her, "freezing her into the mold of a perpetual childhood." She feels that if she remains there, it will be like facing a blank wall for the rest of her life, or like passing thousands of days and nights with nothing to show for them "but the slow stain of unused time." She is sure that the influence of puritanism had acted to contain her father's violent energy, and she imagines the violence of the family sunk like stones beneath the surface of a pond, rigid (corpse-like) beneath a glaze of respectability.

As Lucy wrestles with the problem of whether or not to marry Stephen Lassiter, a violent storm rages outside. Lucy and Jane sit inside with the shutters firmly closed. Jane feels safe and secure, but the storm suggests the life which Jane is attempting to shut out. Before the end of Part One, Lucy has decided to leave Grenville and marry Stephen. She has chosen to live fully and to deny her puritan background which forbids divorce. In New York, alone with Stephen, she remembers a sleigh ride in her childhood when her ears had been badly frozen. She pictures her sheltered life as a child wrapped up against the winter: "Now her whole soul seemed to be unfreezing." Puritanism had originally attempted to shield people from evil, as a child must be protected from the cold. In our own century, MacLennan feels, it has succeeded only in blighting or killing what it had attempted to preserve.

Each of MacLennan's early novels uses houses to symbolize puritan and non-puritan characteristics in their owners. The Wain family house in *Barometer Rising*, described as being typical of the history and character of the town, is forbidding, rather than gracious or beautiful. The shutters have been placed on the inside where they can be useful. Inside, the mood is the same. The furnishings reflect a sombre dignity, not beauty or joy. As an adult, Penny loves only the garden and thinks of the rest of the house as an "incubus." This word, and similar suggestions of a deadening burden or oppressive nightmare, are frequently used by MacLennan in connection with puritanism. The Wain house represents the puritan suspicion of beauty. It is also identified with the stifling, restricting influence which MacLennan associates with puritanism, and suggests by images of blankness and freezing in *The Precipice*. In *Barometer Rising* the heavy oak front door of the Wain mansion, weighted with a brass knocker, is seen by Penny as a symbol: "Her family had shut her in from the world when she was young; it had shut her out from itself when she had ceased being a child." After the death of her father in the explosion, Penny says she can never live in the house again. As she goes with Neil to find Jean, she realizes with a sense of shock that she has left home for the last time. There is a suggestion here of the rebirth-through-death pattern which runs through all MacLennan's novels.

The Cameron house in Grenville has passed through two stages. Under Lucy's father there had been neither gardens nor colour, only blistered tan paint and unsoftened lines. Since it is exactly the kind of house that old John Knox Cameron would choose to live in, its harshness is identified with his character. An earlier Scot had added the brown paint and the harshness. MacLennan describes the Scotch and Scotch-Irish as roughening everything they touched: "It would be another hundred years before any part of English-speaking Canada could hope to be rid of what they had done to it." (Little did

MacLennan suspect, in 1948, what Canada would be like in a mere twenty years.)

Under Lucy's care, the imposed ugliness has been stripped off, and the house transformed. Now beautiful and gracious, it is described as being the outward expression of her personality. MacLennan thus uses the house to show both the puritan character of old John Knox and the non-puritan character of Lucy, and to suggest that we must consciously struggle to cleanse ourselves of the puritan aversion to beauty and joy. In *Two Solitudes*, Yardley's farm in the parish of Saint-Marc is a symbol of non-puritan joyous acceptance of life. Yardley is both proud and pleased to see his first crops growing and his animals thriving. The Methuen and McQueen mansions on the Montreal mountain are status symbols of their owners' concern with financial and social success. These houses seem to entomb their occupants and cut them off from life, like the Wain front door.

We have seen how MacLennan emphasizes, in his first three novels, that the Canadian social environment is strongly puritan. His characters are also presented largely in terms of this concept, which is an obsessive concern in MacLennan's first four novels. Each novel has a contrasting set of characters, puritan and non-puritan by his definition, who are for or against life. The plot structures in *Two Solitudes* and *The Precipice* depend upon a clash of values between these opposing groups. In *Barometer Rising*, puritanism is less important to the structure, which is tightly built around the historic explosion of 1917 in Halifax harbour. Puritan characters have a relatively minor part here, as compared to their major role in the next three novels. Penny's relations, Uncle Alfred and Aunt Maria, are lightly and humorously sketched. They are shown as narrow-minded and self-righteous. Just enough details are given to explain why it is that Penny cannot bear to be alone with them when she is feeling depressed. Alfred's chief interest is the Presbyterian church in which he is an elder, and his chief talent, the ability to estimate the collection value of any congregation to within a half-dollar. MacLennan gives us a more modern version of a puritan in Geoffrey Wain. Wain is a materialist who despises his nephew Neil for his lack of interest in money, and a hypocrite who pays lip service to one sexual code while practising another. Wain's contempt for his mistress Evelyn is really based upon a contempt for sex. These life-denying puritan characters are set in opposition to the hero and heroine of *Barometer Rising*, who affirm life in a spirit of generosity and optimism.

In *Two Solitudes* the puritan values of Janet Methuen, of the Methuen "tribe" in general, and of the Calvinist businessmen such as McQueen and Irons, are opposed to those of the non-puritan characters such as Kathleen Tallard, Captain Yardley, Heather Methuen and Paul Tallard. Athanase Tallard, a character in conflict, has both puritan and non-puritan characteristics.

The prevailing attitudes of the puritan town of Grenville, represented primarily by Jane Cameron, her father old John Knox Cameron, and his aunts, are contrasted with the non-puritan behaviour of Lucy Cameron and her uncle, Matt McCunn. Lucy's family background is given in some detail. Her father had been brought up by two maiden aunts who had made his life a "Calvinistic horror," forbidding him toys as a child and making him afraid of his sex when he grew older. The efforts of these two Scots had apparently been only too successful, for as an adult "John Knox had been hard even for an Ontario small town to take, where the Scotch-Irish are chocolate-brown with Calvinism."

Stephen Lassiter, like Athanase Tallard, is ambivalent. At first sight he appears to be free of puritan inhibitions, and he regards the Grenville attitudes towards drink and sex with amused condescension. It later appears to Lucy that Stephen, even when drunk and in bed with another woman, is more of a puritan than she herself has ever been. Stephen, like her sister Jane, cannot accept weakness in himself. Both are terrified of appearing to be weak or in error; both refuse to accept the Christian promise of forgiveness of sin; both are shown as being obsessed with guilt. Even when they no longer believe in God, as Marcia points out, the old guilt-habit stays. MacLennan has described his intention in *The Precipice* as an attempt to find "a common denominator between U.S. and Canadian tradition which I believe exists in the Puritan background of both countries."[3] The prefatory note in this novel refers to the journey "which the puritans began more than three hundred years ago when they lost hope in themselves and decided to bet their lives on the things they could do rather than the men they were." This restless, discontented urge to accomplish ever greater feats is seen by MacLennan as a drive towards nothingness – hence the title image.

Jane is described as being Grenville's collective conscience. Most of the town's inhabitants make sensible compromises with their puritan code; Jane does not:

She was the only one of them who followed, in thought and life, all the principles of the religion and morality which the entire Protestant part of the country professed to honor. The great crimes had no reality for her whatever. She had never in her life seen an act of deliberate wickedness. It was quite natural for her to believe that sex was the dirtiest thing in the world, and near to the root of all evil. (*P* 122)

Jane loves music and plays well herself. Lucy marvels that anyone could enjoy music as Jane obviously does and yet still consider it unimportant. Jane's attitude reflects the puritan suspicion of beauty and the puritan emphasis on utility. As Lucy listens to Jane's playing she becomes aware of a deep and repressed passion of which Jane herself is unaware. Jane's unconscious sexual frustration is revealed in her playing of the Beethoven "Appassionata": "One would expect her to be at her best in a Bach fugue, but it was only in these slow movements of Beethoven, where religion mingled with a deeply sublimated sexuality, that Jane really found herself in music." (*P* 119)

The hypocrisy of the contemporary puritan attitude towards sex is revealed in the talk between Jane and Lucy after they have learned from a neighbour that Stephen is already married. Jane is concerned with keeping up the appearance of respectability, rather than with truth. Lucy insists that she has done nothing of which she should be ashamed, but Jane paints such a vivid picture of whispering gossipmongers that Lucy is reduced to shame. Lucy is represented in Part One as being slightly puritanical, in MacLennan's sense, in so far as she has not been able to completely purge herself of the fear of sex implanted in her in childhood. She is pictured as making a determined effort to use her mind to free herself from this fear, "fear of nothing but what people like Father put into our minds when we were helpless children."[4] Despite her efforts to overcome her puritanism, Lucy is shocked to discover that Stephen is married and that his attitude towards divorce is extremely casual. Her whole background denies the possibility of her marriage to such a man, and she struggles to discard "the superstitious sense of taboo under which she had been reared." Matt McCunn, her uncle, encourages her to marry Stephen. Like Captain Yardley in *Two Solitudes*, Matt is a vigorous, tolerant and happy man who accepts life. Lucy remembers that in her childhood her whole world had seemed larger whenever Matt had come to their house.

Janet Methuen, in *Two Solitudes*, is very similar to Jane Cameron. Janet and Jane represent the puritan attitudes which MacLennan sees in Canada, "a land still so near the frontier that in most of it everything was black or white, uncomplicated, where wickedness was barely intelligible unless it were sexual." (*TS* 182) When Janet receives word of the death of her husband overseas, her puritan belief that emotions must be restrained and hidden makes her struggle to face the villagers as if nothing had happened. She returns to Yardley's farmhouse and retires to her bedroom. Unfortunately for Janet, the walls are thin and she can overhear the story which her father is telling the Tallards. Yardley's humorous anecdote of the horses and their two "hard-shell" Baptist owners, and Janet's neurotic hysterical reaction to this anecdote, set the puritan and non-puritan attitudes in stark relief. Yardley relates that Calvin Slipp, owner of the stallion "Okay," had "hated Luther's guts" ever since Luther, owner of the mare, had beaten him to the position of church deacon. Under cover of the noise of a Baptist prayer meeting, the two horses are brought together. Janet has been listening upstairs with mounting feelings of horror and embarrassment, and she finally climaxes Yardley's story with hysterical screams.

Yardley, whom Paul later describes as "just a natural man," accepts the idea of sex as normal and natural for both people and animals. Janet does not. When he suggests to her that she should remarry, she calls his suggestion horrible, and considers his idea that "people are not so different even from animals" to be so peculiar as to verge on insanity. When her father is near death, Janet sits by his side from a sense of duty, afraid to show her feelings, for fear of seeming sentimental. Yardley thinks, sadly, that she has been worried about something ever since he could remember, and he is afraid that it is partly his fault. Perhaps if he had had a better education, she would have respected him more, and he would have been able to teach her to find enjoyment in life. "But her mother had made the child ashamed of him, and then her own conscience had made her ashamed of being ashamed, and after that there was no end to the impasse between them." (*TS* 308)

In opposition to the puritan attitudes represented most strikingly by Janet Methuen and Jane Cameron, MacLennan affirms the value of beauty and pleasure. But let no one think that his aversion to puritanism has turned him into an advocate of free love. In no other connection does MacLennan's serious moral attitude towards life show more clearly than in his idea of mature sexual love. In *The Precipice*, he defines mature love as being "a matter of endurance, a matter of wisdom and care." From his novels it is clear that he believes sexual relations should involve the whole person and should entail permanent ties and responsibility. MacLennan's first three novels suggest that feminine beauty reflects moral character, that beauty and goodness are intimately connected in a woman. His heroines (Penny Wain, Heather Methuen, Lucy Cameron) are all women whose beauty of character has had a transforming effect upon their external appearance. Similarly, in each of these novels MacLennan shows women whose beauty is simply physical. The surface beauty of these women – Wain's mistress Evelyn, Daphne Methuen, Nina Cameron, Stephen's first wife Joyce, and his mistress Gail Beaumont – does not reflect any corresponding beauty of spirit. MacLennan believes that beauty without goodness is unsatisfying.

Penny Wain, who fancies herself to be plain, is described as being transformed by contact with another person: "In conversation her face opened and disclosed a sympathetic and comprehensive mind." The heroine of *Two Solitudes* discovers her own beauty in Paul Tallard's eyes after they have fallen in love. Earlier, Paul has reacted with scornful amusement to Heather's admiring description of her honey-blond sister Daphne: "It must be a full-time job, being Daffy." Daphne has been shown to resemble her mother Janet, being cold, hard and priggish, even as a child. After Daphne's marriage to the titled Englishman, Noel Fletcher, Heather realizes that she has been foolish to admire and envy Daphne for her beauty. She now sees her sister's beauty as a weapon, a destiny, her only wealth. Suddenly, Heather feels freed from her lifelong dependence upon her sister. She judges Noel and Daphne, and condemns their whole attitude towards life: "They had nothing whatever she wanted, for all they possessed was a cold surface beauty and his ability, motivated by a mechanical sensuality, to counterfeit the fire she knew was still alive in the world, somewhere, if she could find it." (*TS* 256)

The love which Heather and Paul have for one another embodies MacLennan's idea of mature love, where sex is part, but only part, of a total relationship. Paul and Heather have no sooner met, as adults, and fallen in love, than MacLennan separates them physically for five years. During this separation their mental and spiritual intimacy continues to grow. She is not afraid to open to him in letters, so that he feels towards the end of this period that he knows her better than when he left Canada. Just before his return, an incident in Athens reveals MacLennan's moral attitude towards sex. A German strength-through-joy ship is in port. Paul watches a German Nazi with an attractive French woman at a nearby café table. Paul despises the German for his crudity and considers casual sexual relationships only another form of loneliness. After Paul and Heather are married, he tells her that his love is "for always."

In *The Precipice*, Stephen tells Lucy she is "simple and decent and lovely." He finds her to be beautiful in a way that few women are any more, and he contrasts her beauty with the soulless sophisticated beauty of his first wife. He asks Lucy if she thinks, seeing Joyce's picture, that she could be generous or warm. Lucy's sister Nina is depicted, like Joyce, as vain and self-seeking. Lucy fears that Nina will only make Bruce more restless, instead of helping him. Stephen tells Lucy that Nina will never get what she wants because she will never give enough, and that "Nina is the last girl, as a type, that a wise man would choose to go to bed with." After the war we see Stephen's prophecy coming true. Nina's dissatisfaction and unhappiness are caused by her selfishness, which is actually spoiling her physical beauty.

There are five main scenes in *Barometer Rising* which are concerned with sexual relationships. In some of these the lovers have MacLennan's approval, while in others they do not. His underlying attitude as to the proper and improper use of sex is shown indirectly but clearly. In the first such scene, on Sunday evening in the Wain house, Angus Murray and Penny Wain are somewhat inhibited, and MacLennan might be accused of puritanism under his own definition. Penny, although twenty-nine and a mother, is shy, "daintily awkward" as a young colt. The inhibitions of this scene reflect the author's moral attitude. He cannot approve of sexual relations between these two, for Penny is to be reunited with Neil. (Yet in the Canadian social climate of the forties, the sheer fact that Penny has had a child out of wedlock is sufficient to make MacLennan very much the *immoral* moralist. Alec Lucas notes that Penny's child was responsible for keeping *Barometer Rising* out of many a school, and that the love scenes in *Two Solitudes*, conservative as they now appear, were so daring at the time as to give rise to the request that the author give the reader notice in future when similar sinful situations were pending, so that they might be skipped over.[5])

In the second scene, Mamie, the madam of a brothel, has the author's approval because she represents *agape* or unselfish concern for the welfare of others. As she tries to help Murray out of his depressed mood, her face is kindly. She criticizes her girls for not caring, and she uses her earnings to support her children in the countryside. MacLennan uses Murray's drunkenness as a technical device for introducing prophecy: "'Though I speak with the tongues of men and of angels and have not charity' – his voice broke – 'Mamie, you're a good girl. . . . You just want us all to be one big happy family.'" (*BR* 136)

The next two love scenes consist of two pairs of incidents set in a curious counterpoint. The married love of Jim and Mary Fraser, who genuinely and deeply care for one another, is set against the relationship of Geoffrey Wain and his mistress Evelyn, who despise each other. Wain considers Evelyn his social inferior, and despises her vulgarity. Evelyn hates Wain and uses sex as a weapon for material advancement. MacLennan emphasizes their mutual scorn and disdain. The scene in Evelyn's apartment is followed immediately by a short scene in Prince's Lodge, where Jim and Mary Fraser have a teasing but loving conversation before their "rendezvous in bed."

Shortly after, MacLennan shows both couples on the following morning. In one short paragraph describing Wain waking in Evelyn's bed, MacLennan preaches a sermon on the undesirability of sex divorced from love:

To Geoffrey Wain, the sunlight coming in through Evelyn's faded lace curtains . . . was vaguely insulting. . . . Evelyn had fallen asleep naked, too lazy to put on the nightgown she had discarded over the side of the bed. . . . The deadness of expression caused by sleep robbed her of all attractiveness. Her slightness . . . now seemed a defect . . . her breath had an odour of acetone which displeased him too, although it never occurred to him that in this respect he was the greater offender. (*BR* 146-7)

Why should the sunlight be insulting? Why should Evelyn be condemned as "lazy"? MacLennan's moral disapproval colours every line of this paragraph. He shows that nothing is really attractive or pleasurable, and that there is neither beauty nor joy in such a relationship. The view of untidy backyards and garbage which Wain sees out the window is identified with the affair. By contrast, the sunlight which the Frasers enjoy with their breakfast is not insulting, but dazzling, brilliant. They are happy as they eat breakfast together and argue good-naturedly on their way to the train. The parallel structure serves as an indirect comment on the use and abuse of sex.

Finally, there is the love which Penny Wain and Neil MacRae have for one another. This love has been consummated before Neil went overseas. Both Penny and Neil relive it in memory. For Penny, the experience had a quality almost sacramental: "into thy hands I commend my spirit." Neil remembers the peonies by their bed, full-blown and fragrant, a symbol of consummated love. There is no inhibition in MacLennan's handling of this love scene. The description is both passionate and delicate. The lovers, although unmarried at the time, seem to be permanently committed to one another by their act. As Penny and Neil go together to find Jean at Prince's Lodge in the last chapter, Penny feels that she is tied to

Neil, "a prisoner of his maleness because once she had wanted him and he had refused to forget it." Their difficult progress through the dark night becomes for Penny a symbol of the inevitability of the permanence of their relationship. Why inevitable? There is no apparent necessity in the events themselves, although Jean's foster parents have been conveniently disposed of. The inevitability follows from MacLennan's ethic, that sexual relations should mean permanent and total involvement of the whole person.

Compare this with Lucy Cameron's relations with Steve Lassiter. Their wedding night is distanced by placing it in Lucy's memory, as with the Montreal love scene in *Barometer Rising*. In *The Precipice*, as in the earlier novel, there is a sense of reverence towards the experience, a sense of wonder and joy. Even after several years of marriage, Lucy maintains her feeling of wonder and gratitude for her position as Stephen's wife, and for his physical candour which has effaced the last traces of puritan shame she has brought with her into marriage. Against the puritan attitude of condemnation MacLennan affirms, like D.H. Lawrence, that sex is good and is to be enjoyed with reverence and thankfulness.

But only under certain conditions. When Lucy thinks of Stephen and Gail together, the violence of her imagination makes her actually shake. She imagines scenes, "natural as health were she a part of them, obscene and terrible and unjust when they were of Stephen and Gail." Sexual relations, then, are to be considered natural as health, or obscene and terrible and unjust, depending on the context. On the next page, Marcia relates an anecdote about multiple marriages and the resulting confusion for the children of such marriages. Lucy recoils in horror. Her children must never be subject to this. Whereas earlier she had spoken broadly and tolerantly of forgiving adultery, even of expecting it in a man such as Stephen, she now realizes that she cannot live long in a state of suspense and dishonesty. Although these remarks belong to dramatic fictional situations, the entire context convinces the reader that Lucy's opinions are also MacLennan's. Marital fidelity is depicted as being necessary for psychological health.

Two Solitudes reveals the same underlying attitude towards sex as the earlier novels. Kathleen has spent the night with Athanase Tallard at the time of his first wife's death. He is convinced that she is thereby responsible for his renewed will to live. And he knows that he will always be grateful to her for this. They are married, but later cease to interest one another, since the marriage has been based more on sexual attraction than on their whole personalities.

Earlier, when Athanase had been rejected physically by his first wife, he had found that he could be neither "a celibate nor a cynical boulevardier." Athanase is seeking the permanent and complete union which MacLennan holds up as the ideal. It is part of Athanase's tragedy that he fails to find happiness in marriage, as he fails to find it in other areas of his life.

There are two exceptions in the early novels to MacLennan's general attitude towards sex as involving a permanent commitment. In *Two Solitudes*, there is the encounter in a Montreal hotel between Kathleen and the strange officer Dennis Morey. Secondly, there is an incident in *The Precipice* where Nina refuses to spend the night with a young airman in Halifax. MacLennan indicates that she should have done so. Nina is condemned for failing to meet a human need, the boy's excessive fear and loneliness. These episodes are not in MacLennan's general pattern. Both might be described as versions of the New Morality, where each individual situation must be judged uniquely by love's concern for another's need. Kathleen tells herself that her encounter with Morey has happened in accordance with some deep necessity, "that even though for others it might be a sin, for her at this particular time it had been good." MacLennan made Morey his mouthpiece for a violent attack on Canadian puritanism, and perhaps felt compelled to let the situation arrive at its logical conclusion. In the next chapter, Kathleen remembers her husband and son, and wonders if her act has harmed them. It is probable that her doubts here echo MacLennan's own uneasiness with the situation.

The incident may also have a bearing upon MacLennan's rejection of Kathleen in the later parts of the novel. In Part One, Kathleen is presented as amoral rather than immoral; her movements are sexually provocative, but are also "of an earthy gentleness, almost of a strangely individual innocence." She is described as being easy-going and accepting. By working as a hat-check girl in a hotel, she is fulfilling herself, using her one talent which is to be herself. Both her son Paul and her husband Athanase depend heavily upon her. When she has been absent in Montreal, Paul feels her return makes the world once again gay and full of wonder. Athanase has credited her with renewing his will to live on the night his first wife died.

In contrast to this earlier treatment, MacLennan's later treatment of Kathleen is strangely scornful and condescending. After Athanase's death she seems no longer admirable. Her fragrance, warmth and softness, once so wonderful to Paul, are now unable to relieve his loneliness. Kathleen leaves the dishes unwashed and the beds unmade while she seeks enjoyment outside the apartment; and Paul, left to find his own amusement, does these jobs for her. Paul feels that she is "still herself yet somehow much less than she had been before." Her smile, although sincere, is "still somehow automatic." Why is MacLennan, a most careful writer with regard to style, reduced to using the word "somehow" twice in consecutive sentences? I suggest that it is the author's moral bias, suppressed earlier, now rising to reject Kathleen. Thirteen years later, at her second marriage, Paul finds the ceremony shocking: "The food being blessed was stale; indeed it had already been eaten." Kathleen and her new husband, Henry Clayton, have already lived together for some time, and MacLennan's condemnation of this is symbolized by the ugliness of the physical conditions of their marriage: the background traffic noise, the excessive heat and humidity, the ink-blotted register. Paul tells himself that his attitude is senseless, but he cannot change it, and Kathleen's parting words are a request for her son's forgiveness. MacLennan's rejection of Kathleen, in the second and third parts of *Two Solitudes*, is one of the most striking examples of the ambivalence which results from his refusal to see any connection between the puritanism which he is attacking and his own moral values.

With the single two exceptions discussed above, MacLennan's early novels condemn casual sexual relations. The behaviour of a man like Noel Fletcher, which might appear as unpuritanical and thereby liable to MacLennan's approval, is condemned as "mechanical sensuality." The relations of Gail Beaumont and Stephen Lassiter are "obscene and terrible and unjust." In MacLennan's serious and moral definition, the right use of sex is part of a total and permanent relationship. Only within this context is sex natural as health. With MacLennan, as with the historic Puritans, morality is the first concern.

NOTES

1. See N.O. Brown, *Life Against Death* (Middletown, Conn.: Wesleyan University Press, 1970), p. 86 and *passim*.

2. D.H. Lawrence, "The Crown," *Reflections on the Death of a Porcupine and Other Essays* (Bloomington: Indiana University Press, 1963), p. 6.

3. Quoted in Hugo McPherson, "The Novels of Hugh MacLennan," *Queen's Quarterly*, 60 (1953-4), 193. See also George Woodcock, *Hugh MacLennan*, Studies in Canadian Literature 5 (Toronto: Copp Clark, 1969), pp. 85-6: "The great balancing act which MacLennan attempts in *The*

Precipice is to demonstrate that Jane and Stephen, who detest each other and seem poles apart, are really siblings under the skin. . . ."

4. Cf. MacLennan's letter to John Gray, 1951, quoted in Note 9 to Chapter Three.

5. See Alec Lucas, *Hugh MacLennan*, Canadian Writers No. 8 (Toronto: McClelland and Stewart, 1970), p. 17. Lucas adds a further example of the reaction provoked by MacLennan's novels in the forties, when they were blamed in the *Presbyterian Recorder* for destroying the morality of the nation: "MacLennan stood his ground and, threatening a lawsuit, drove his adversary to seek refuge in a polished, though tepid, retraction."

5 MACLENNAN'S EARLY NOVELS: WORK

Calvinism, as we have seen, denies in theory that man could win salvation by his works. In practice, however, an emphasis on the moral value and the social necessity of hard work was deeply engrained in the Puritan character. Calvin had glorified the work of the business financier, and Luther, that of the peasant craftsman. All of the Puritan groups were motivated by a reforming, improving urge in relation to society. This same intention can be seen in MacLennan's novels as supplying a basic motivation in his characters.

One feels a strange tension and ambivalence in MacLennan's attitude towards work. On the one hand, his essays attack the ideal of hard work as materialistic; his novels satirize the ideal through characters such as McQueen, Sir Rupert Irons, Henry Clayton, Abel and Stephen Lassiter; and his prefatory note to *The Precipice* speaks of the historic Puritans losing hope in themselves, and trusting only in their accomplishments. Despite this attack, we find on closer inspection that MacLennan's heroes and heroines all work very hard indeed – and they do so, for the most part, with MacLennan's obvious blessing. Hard work and self-discipline turn out to be necessary after all. MacLennan's intellect and emotions cannot deny this Puritan ethic.

In *Barometer Rising*, work is praised and attacked by turn. On the one hand, an obsession with work is seen as an escape from or denial of life; as such, it is part of MacLennan's definition of the puritanism which he is attacking. Penny Wain, alone and depressed before she knows of Neil MacRae's return, thinks that the "anaesthetic" of hard work cannot compensate for the feeling of life and growth that she has lost. "Like a man in the desert obsessed by thoughts of green grass and running water," she remembers things from before the war, remembers dancing, and the heavy odour of lime trees in the streets. Later, when she is convalescing after her injury from the explosion, she condemns her life of the past few years as ridiculous, because she has spent it pretending to herself that her sole ambition was to succeed in a "man's profession." When Angus Murray tells Penny that it is no use their continuing to go on as they have been doing, Penny offers her work as an excuse for her self-sufficiency. Murray refuses to accept this excuse, and denies that Penny can be happy or fulfilled through work alone. The quick fear in Penny's eyes shows that the author, like Murray, condemns her attempt to escape from a full life by means of work.

On the other hand, there are many passages where the desire to work is treated affirmatively by MacLennan. Angus Murray, after he has ordered Penny's Aunt Maria to turn the Wain house into an emergency hospital, says that the old woman will be in her element in this situation. Aunt Maria's devotion to work and duty is depicted as positive and good. The puritan town of Halifax undergoes a similar metamorphosis. MacLennan, praising the high morale of the townsfolk as they struggle with the terrible aftermath of the explosion, describes Halifax as "cashing in on a century of unconscious self-discipline." (*BR* 181) Similarly, Neil describes Halifax as a "good town," telling Penny that professional soldiers could have been demoralized by a lot less than these people have endured. For Murray, Neil's return means that he has lost all hope of marrying Penny. Murray experiences, first, a severe depression and, second, a sort of rebirth, in which the chief thing he looks forward to with joy is the prospect of being able to work again. His fingers were recovering and soon would be fit. His work would have to be enough from now on. When Penny leaves Murray after having told him she is Jean's mother, her desire to work is presented in almost mystical terms. She wants more than anything else to be left alone, "alone with the absolute and unquestioning simplicity of figures and the docile beauty of white lines on blue paper. . . . Once again she was the capable technician." (*BR* 78)

Work, in the final analysis, is intimately connected with moral duty. And moral duty is a basic concern of the characters whom MacLennan presents for our admiration. Penny, although economically independent, remains in her father's house because of her concern for her young brother. When Murray asks her why she remains in a house she hates, Penny explains that she cannot abandon Roddie to their unsympathetic and puritanical family. Similarly, it is Penny's concern for Neil's welfare that had made her refuse to marry him before he had gone overseas. Their marriage would have made his existence as one of her father's subordinates even more difficult than it was bound to be. Penny's three years of secrecy and self-denial have been suffered voluntarily for Neil's sake. Murray's admiration for Penny in this situation reflects MacLennan's own admiration for self-denial undergone for the sake of others. After the explosion, both Neil and Murray are labouring under physical handicaps. Murray forces his injured hand to be "adequate" for the medical tasks required of him, and Neil makes his injured leg "equal to the task" of carrying Penny. In a word, they do their duty.

The heroes in MacLennan's novels are ship designers, architects, doctors, engineers. Even the heroine, in *Barometer Rising*, is a ship designer, described as one of the most brilliant women in Canada. Two of his heroines, Heather Methuen and Catherine Martell, are artists. But although Catherine plays an important role in *The Watch That Ends the Night*, the dominating figure is that of Jerome, the doctor. Why this concentration on practical professions in the novels of a man who professes to condemn action as materialistic? These are the professions of men who wish to improve society and who like to combine utility with beauty. As a ship designer, Neil's dreams of excellence are never satisfied. He glories in the old Nova Scotian tradition of fine craftsmanship, and fears it will be lost in mass production: "Vessels in crates, and the devil with quality." He despises the new social attitudes which downgrade craftsmanship and concentrate on manipulating men. There are similar attacks on the evils of mass production in the essays. MacLennan's economic ideals are closer to those of Luther than of Calvin. Calvin appreciated the importance of money in the economy at large, and approved of the businessman who spent his life manipulating money. Geoffrey Wain condemns Neil for being completely impractical, by which Wain means that Neil is not interested in making money. Neil, an idealist, is interested only in designing ships. And it is Neil, not Wain, who has MacLennan's approval.

In *Two Solitudes*, the Montreal Protestant business community, represented by McQueen and Sir Rupert Irons, is used by MacLennan to satirize the Calvinist ideal of the businessman as God's faithful steward. MacLennan descends almost to farce in his description of the businessmen waiting for the elevator. They are all dressed alike (very conservatively); they are all "sound" in their business policy; all Presbyterians, all regular churchgoers. Irons is known to believe quite literally in predestination. The description of Irons at the time of his funeral reads like a parody of the Calvinist business ideals described by R.H. Tawney. Irons has always avoided ostentation, has furnished his home with the barest of necessities, and has never taken a holiday, "in order to reserve his powers for the fuller service to mankind that his wealth had demanded." MacLennan's choice of a name is interesting in this respect, as Tawney describes the new middle class of the sixteenth and seventeenth centuries, in which Calvinism took root most deeply, as "a race of iron."[1]

Huntly McQueen, like Irons, aspires to public service. His voice assumes an evangelical tone as he explains to Athanase Tallard that he is interested in more than money, that he wants to see the country properly developed. Later, he decides that his dreams of organizing the entire country were too grandiose. He plans instead to endow a Presbyterian theological college in his will. He considers himself to be a self-made man, and condemns the poor as lazy. When McQueen is exasperated by the world crisis of 1939, by the dangers which it poses to his business and the inconveniences it entails in his personal life, he rages silently: "So he was decadent, was he? . . . He had worked hard all his life, had saved his money, had never got drunk or gone with women." Throughout the novel, MacLennan shows that to refrain from doing these things is just so much too little in the battle of life. He shows that Irons and McQueen are selfish and egotistical and utterly without love. McQueen's emotional attachment, after the death of his mother, seems to be limited to his cat. The cat, plump, placid and self-satisfied, is identified with McQueen. The financial soundness upon which these men pride themselves means, in the last analysis, a care for their own interests and a shrewd ability to protect these interests. When Athanase Tallard is comparing English- and French-Canadians, he thinks that the production, acquisition and distribution of wealth is the English-Canadian's only purpose. The author depicts the Calvinist businessman as at best materialistic, and at worst hypocritical, for his vaunted public service is really the protecting of his own interests. MacLennan, like Captain Yardley, "never could take fellas like McQueen seriously."

Since the Calvinist businessman, however, may intend, like the architect or the doctor, to serve society, and since a return to a natural rather than a money economy is impossible for the modern world, MacLennan's attack on this type must appear inconsistent and somewhat unfair. MacLennan seems to be unable to see this type as anything but hypocritical and materialistic.

The attack on Henry Clayton, who marries Paul's widowed mother Kathleen, reflects a similar line of thought. Although thinly veiled as the thoughts and feelings of Paul, the scorn for Clayton is clearly MacLennan's own. Life to Clayton is fun and business: "business consisted in making money and moving large objects from one place to another. Beyond production and profit he never thought an inch. He believed that the more mechanical equipment a man has at his disposal, the better and happier he is. No man could have too many gadgets, the world could never weary of working its life away producing labour-saving devices." (*TS* 250) Paul's condescension and scorn are clear when Kathleen promises that her husband can get Paul a job, and Paul ironically inquires as to what kind of a job Mr. Clayton might offer.

The Lassiter businessmen in *The Precipice* are a slightly different breed. Abel Lassiter's father has been a "fierce" Baptist. Abel is no churchgoer, but he often told his son Stephen, "there was nothing better than a Baptist church for putting an edge on a man." (*P* 67) In Abel Lassiter we see the original Puritan drive, to serve God by means of action, turned into a neurotic reflex, a compulsion to work for the sake of work. Abel had reached the point where he refused to hire a man with a happy face. Stephen realizes that his father's chief characteristic had not been intellectual discernment but simply a furious, ultimately uncontrollable drive. Stephen, because of his father's upbringing, fears failure and is haunted by the feeling that he can never be even as successful as his father's subordinates.

Both *Two Solitudes* and *The Precipice*, however, contain a defence of work as necessary and good. Lucy Cameron's garden is presented at first as an anti-puritan symbol of beauty and sheer being. Her flowers have helped to transform John Knox Cameron's house into something beautiful and gracious. They are a source of joy to herself, her family and her neighbours. When Stephen objects that flowers don't lead to much, he is rebuked by Lucy. Flowers exist in their own right, by their own beauty. But MacLennan is unable to leave the garden as a simple symbol of beauty and joy. Lucy has ambitious plans for her garden. She envisages a bigger one, and a business of selling cut flowers in Toronto. Alternately, she longs to breed flowers scientifically, to develop new varieties after the manner of Burbank, a famous botanist whom she admires. She tells Jane that it is silly of her to go on growing flowers just as a hobby when she can do much more. Both of these plans are quite different from the simple enjoyment of beauty in a small garden.

They are not condemned by MacLennan, but are presented as part of Lucy's urge to live a full life.

The attitude of both Lucy and Stephen towards Stephen's engineering work, and the sharp contrast between this and Carl's advertising business, reveals MacLennan's preference for engineering. Lucy, Marcia and Stephen all despise the advertising business. Lucy feels a contemptuous anger for Carl's whole business, as she thinks of his private office where the tooled leather chairs, in Bratian's phrase, are designed to flatter the backsides of prospective customers. She finds Carl a pitiless bore. Marcia speaks of Carl's "lovely business," which functions in order to corrupt America. Carl admits that his business is vulgar, but brilliantly vulgar. Many of his accounts pander to the desire for sexual sophistication which he believes to be part of contemporary culture in America. When his subordinates develop various guilt neuroses, Bratian treats them with tolerant amusement. His own philosophy is that life is completely without meaning, and his own desire is to satisfy his childhood frustrations caused by poverty.

MacLennan's scorn for Carl's cynicism is reflected in the attitudes of Lucy, Marcia and Stephen. Stephen considers it a "lousy" business, but assures himself that it is only a stepping-stone to something better. Meanwhile, his own work at Carl's agency makes use of his engineering knowledge. He tells himself there is a considerable difference between handling an account for the best medium-bomber in his country's air force, and dreaming up seduction scenes for underwear or men's cosmetics. Stephen passionately desires to get back into engineering work. He admires Myron Harper, whose airplane account he handles, and wishes that he had met him earlier in life. He is pleased to be remembered as an engineer by Carson, and shares Carson's conviction that an engineer's business is making things, not writing about the work of others. Lucy approves of Carson, who never appears before the reader in person, but who carries a mystical aura of goodness. She tells Stephen that Carson is everything that Carl is not, and that if he worked for a man like that everything would seem different: "There's death in a man like Carl. Ultimately he kills whatever he touches."

Lucy admires Stephen's factual engineer's mind, so different from her own. She envisages a model town in California which would depend upon the knowledge and ability of engineers, "a garden of fruit and flowers belonging to Stephen and herself in a land which once had been a desert but now was the richest growing country on earth, watered by a great and distant dam which Stephen himself, even in the smallest possible way, had helped to build." (*P* 278)

When Stephen is about to leave Lucy at the end of the novel, his future has been left unresolved by MacLennan, and yet it seems clear that Stephen wants to work with his hands and, eventually, in engineering. Stephen's desire for this type of work obviously has the author's approval. It is only Stephen's tendency to take upon himself "a devious, useless punishment for a useless, ancient guilt" which is condemned by MacLennan as puritan, negative and repressive. Similarly, Marcia finds fulfilment for the first time in her adult life in the hard work of a hospital nursing aide. She is proud of her work's being accepted and recognized by the doctors and nurses whom she admires.

In *Two Solitudes*, Athanase Tallard has a vision of a model community, which is similar to Lucy's ideal, in *The Precipice*. He intends to use the factory in Saint-Marc as the foundation of a rebuilt parish, where improved living standards give everyone a chance. The factory will enable the town to have a model school, a hospital, a public library, a playground and, finally, a theatre. Later, when Athanase has been frustrated in his attempt to share with McQueen in the building of the factory, he plans to endow a public library and set it up in the French section of Montreal: "Did the priests think they had a monopoly on public service?" This dream-vision of Athanase's suggests that work and money can be used positively for the good of the community.

In Heather, Paul and Yardley, the novel's other main characters, work is also seen as something good. Moreover, these are all characters whom MacLennan has established as being basically non-puritan in his sense. Heather is described as having missed regular work greatly since she has left the university. She works seriously at her painting, in the face of family opposition. They consider it a minor hobby. She feels that if it is her economic duty to be useless, then capitalism is obviously all wrong. Paul, after his mother's second marriage, feels that he has things he must do, and that a lifetime will not be long enough to do them properly. Paul's work is eulogized through Heather's thoughts: "She loved him so utterly he had become her way of life. For a man it could never be the same. He had his work, he had the ruthless drive inside him that would never let him alone." (*TS* 321)[2] Paul's dedication to his work of writing, despite the difficulties which this creates for his personal life, is presented by MacLennan as admirable.

Captain Yardley has worked hard all his life: first at sea; later, in his farm in the parish of Saint-Marc. In his spare time, he reads serious books, plays chess and carves ship models. In old age, when physical work has become impossible for him, Yardley works with his mind, taking university extension courses. Unlike Dr. Ainslie's study of Greek, Yardley's studying is not presented as obsessive or compulsive. He thinks "that perhaps after all there was something ostentatious in a man like himself studying Greek. . . . It was partly a sense of humour that had made him start it anyway." (*TS* 270)

We find, then, a curious ambivalence in MacLennan's attitude towards the value of work. On the one hand, he tends to condemn it as materialistic and to suggest that it may be used as an escape from life. Sir Rupert Irons' or Huntly McQueen's preoccupation with business and Janet Methuen's exhausting war work are examples of work that MacLennan considers to stem from negative attitudes. Both McQueen and Stephen Lassiter refer to their work in an attempt to justify themselves in time of trouble. Stephen, alone and jobless in a Chicago hotel, asks why he should be in such a fix: "Christ, it wasn't as if he hadn't worked hard all his life!" In these instances, the ideal of hard work is satirized and condemned by MacLennan.

On the other hand, MacLennan gives his approval to the constructive work of the architect and ship designer, the engineer, the doctor and the writer. His fictional heroes are all hard workers, although some of them must learn that work is not to be done in an effort to earn forgiveness for sins. Old Dr. MacKenzie, whom Ainslie admires so deeply, is a tremendous worker, still active at the age of seventy-six. The hospital owes its very existence to his energy and determination. But Dr. MacKenzie works without guilt and without frustration. Captain Yardley also continues to work to the end of a full, rich life. Both men remain Presbyterians to the end of their lives.

MacLennan's heroes tend to go in pairs – a thinker and a doer. Angus Murray, the philosophic doctor in *Barometer Rising*, saves Neil MacRae by getting the dying Alec to sign a paper necessary to establish Neil's innocence. Neil, immersed in action, has totally neglected this. Bruce Fraser, the intellectual and idealist, is contrasted with Stephen the engineer; but it is Stephen's factual engineer's mind, so totally different from her own, that Lucy most admires. The quiet contemplative personality of George Stewart is contrasted with the startling figure of Jerome Martell, doctor and soldier. And Daniel Ainslie's tragedy is paralleled by that of Archie MacNeil, the boxer. The pattern varies in *Two Solitudes*, where both Athanase and his son Paul are thinkers, as well as being men of action; but only in Paul are the conflicting tendencies resolved successfully into a strong and confident character. These pairs of heroes, taken together, might represent man's ability to think and act. Each man, of course, does both. The difference is one of emphasis. The "doer" is himself a contemplative in most cases, as with Jerome, Ainslie, Dr. MacKenzie and Paul Tallard. MacLennan's heroines follow a similar pattern. His admiration obviously rests with these men and women whose professions are dedicated to the service of mankind. His condemnation of action as negative and repressive is contradicted by the main characters in all of his novels. How then do we explain his ambivalence in this regard? I suggest that the clue lies in the attitude which the individual has towards his work. Work undertaken in a spirit of joy and self-fulfilment, and constructive work which benefits society, is seen by MacLennan as positive and good. Work undertaken in a martyr spirit, as with Janet Methuen, or in an attempt to earn forgiveness for guilt (as Lucy interprets Stephen's work), is seen by MacLennan as negative and bad.

MacLennan's attitude towards work compares interestingly with the treatment of work in the writings of Norman O. Brown and Herbert Marcuse. Karl Marx, in his early works, has a conception of the radical viciousness of the civilized mind, which he terms "the alienated consciousness." Marx correlates this with a money economy, and locates its root in the compulsion to work, a compulsion which subordinates man to things and reduces the drive of the human being to greed and competition. Brown, agreeing with the Marxian condemnation of alienated or unsatisfying work, writes: "Thus the apparent accumulation of wealth is really the impoverishment of human nature, and its appropriate morality is the renunciation of human nature and desires – asceticism."[3] Marcuse, like Brown, believes in the erotization of the entire personality, and views enjoyable work as a sublimated form of Eros. Marcuse favours a culture where the individual exists not as an instrument of alienated labour but as a subject of self-realization: "in other words, if socially useful work is at the same time the transparent satisfaction of an individual need."[4]

What Freud calls repression and Marx, alienated or compulsive work, MacLennan depicts as non-enjoyment, and aligns, in his fiction, with patterns of action and images which negate life. MacLennan's celebration of work, when it is done for the benefit of society and as a necessary fulfilment of the individual's own character, provides a link between the moralism of historical Puritanism and contemporary post-Freudian, post-Marxian thought.

NOTES

1. R.H. Tawney, *Religion and the Rise of Capitalism* (Penguin, 1964), p. 120. The name recurs as an archetype in *The Watch That Ends the Night*, p. 162: "The slums. The insecurity. The whole damned nineteenth century set-up Sir Rupert Irons represents."

2. It is interesting to note the male chauvinism in this remark, the assumption that the professional work-drive is restricted to men. One doubts whether such a remark would be made a generation later amid the voices of Women's Lib.

3. Norman O. Brown, *Life Against Death* (Middletown, Conn.: Wesleyan University Press, 1970), p. 238.

4. Herbert Marcuse, "Sexuality into Eros," *The New Eroticism*, ed. Philip Nobile (New York: Random House, 1970), p. 25.

6 'THE NEED AND THE ALLNESS OF LOVE'

The "ancient curse" described in the Author's Note to *Each Man's Son* has been referred to as the key to MacLennan's conception of modern puritanism. The curse is the puritan's sense of shame and guilt. The Note prepares the reader to see in the protagonist, Daniel Ainslie, a man continually haunted by a sense of sin, the legacy of the ancient curse. Within the novel, MacLennan mounts a major attack on this legacy through the words of old Dr. Dougald MacKenzie. Dr. Dougald, Ainslie's teacher and friend, acts as a choric figure to interpret and comment upon the action. He is the only person in the whole of Cape Breton whom Ainslie honours unreservedly, and is clearly the author's spokesman. Dr. Dougald denies that Calvin and his followers should be called Christian.[1] He refers to Calvin's doctrine of man's guilt and damnation, and continues: "I'm a Christian, Dan, but Calvin wasn't one and neither was your father. It may sound ridiculous to say, in cold words, that you feel guilty merely because you are alive, but that's what you were taught to believe until you grew up." (*EMS* 67) Later, he describes the Calvinism of the Lowlanders as making men "ashamed of living."

Daniel Ainslie broods over his revelation. His intellect, like that of Lucy Cameron before marriage, has so far been incapable of freeing him from emotional fears implanted in childhood. He asks himself if he can ever hope to be free of the "circle of Original Sin," and he tries to understand how these fears have acted within his own personal life. He begins to see that his guilt feelings in relation to his desire for his own wife Margaret stem directly from the teachings of his childhood.[2] He has been taught to fear sex because "it led hellward." But Dr. MacKenzie has told him that he is trying to make work compensate for a breakdown in his relationship with his wife, and that he has secretly resented Margaret because she has not been able to wash away his sense of sin. (*EMS* 64, 67) Dr. MacKenzie continues to lead Daniel towards greater self-understanding. He says that the ancient Highlanders "knew as well as Christ did that only the sinner can become the saint because only the sinner can understand the need and the allness of love." (*EMS* 69) The need and the allness of love is the novel's theme.[3]

In the Cape Breton mining town of Broughton, there is a strongly puritan social environment of the Calvinist type which MacLennan abhors. MacLennan himself comes from this area, and his father had a difficult medical practice in a Cape Breton mining town. This explains the sureness and immediacy which comes across in this novel. Old Mrs. MacCuish, Mollie MacNeil's neighbour, is a puritan archetype. She catches Mollie's son Alan alone one day when his mother is not well, and terrifies him as much by her whole personality, forbidding and accusing, as by her threatening prophecies. Alan is unfamiliar with the word "sin," but Mrs. MacCuish assures him that he is himself a lump of it, and may expect to be punished for it hereafter. When Alan has managed to get away from Mrs. MacCuish and her mouldy bitter food, he encounters another neighbour, smiling and pleasant. With Mrs. MacDonald, he feels no fear. The feeling of fear which Mrs. MacCuish engenders in Alan typifies the feeling produced in anyone by the type of puritanism which MacLennan deplores.

In a lighter vein, there are many humorous sketches to fill out the puritan background. The Reverend MacAlistair worries lest his congregation take the promises of the New Testament too literally: "For if God was love, what was to be done about Jehovah?" Jimmie MacGillivray, the saloon-keeper, fears that his recurring stomach-ache may have been sent as a punishment for sin; if so, he sees no hope for relief for he is already doing his utmost to keep the Sabbath holy. His family cooked all the food for Sunday on Saturday, laid it out on the table, and even filled all the glasses in the house with water the night before, "so that not a tap was turned in the Mac-Gillivray house on the Sabbath."

In Dr. Daniel Ainslie, MacLennan shows us a man driven to work compulsively in a frantic effort to free himself from a feeling of shame and guilt, the ancient curse. Subconsciously, Ainslie is attempting to earn forgiveness by hard work. The folly of this attempt is revealed directly in the words of old Dr. MacKenzie, and is also suggested through the depressing, killing nature of the work in the mines. The mines provide a sombre background for the story, and are described by Dr. Ainslie as no more than a corruption. He observes the desperate look of the young men who realize that they have been trapped by the mines for life. The mine's train and trestle appear from a distance as "a column of black ants that had crawled up the stalk of a gigantic plant and died there." The spreading galleries of the mine are compared with the tentacles of an octopus. These images reinforce the description of the mine as a corruption. The anonymity of the workers, their faces blackened with soot, recalls the attacks in MacLennan's essays on factories and mass production methods which endanger the individual personality.

In *Each Man's Son*, as in MacLennan's first three novels, one's first impression is that the author is attacking hard work as neurotic and as a misjudged effort to achieve release from guilt feelings. Daniel Ainslie is introduced to the reader by Mollie MacNeil, as a special man who works so hard that he sometimes misses two or three nights of sleep. To Mollie, he represents a shining figure on a pedestal. She hopes that her son Alan will grow up to be like him. But Ainslie himself knows that he has lost the joy of living which he had as a youth, lost in former eager anticipation of the future: "Now that future was the present, and what had it brought? . . . Just the moment of hard work. The memory of work endlessly hard." (*EMS* 46)

Certain key images help to portray work as neurotic. One such image is that of Sisyphus; another, that of a treadmill; and a third, of flagellation. In Greek legend, Sisyphus was an ancient king of Corinth, condemned in Hades throughout eternity to roll uphill a huge stone that always tumbled down again. Daniel Ainslie sees himself in his own mind as another Sisyphus, endlessly striving to roll the rock uphill, fearful that if he ever relaxes it will roar down to the valley bottom again: "Was defiance all that remained?" (*EMS* 46) *The Watch That Ends the Night* also contains a reference to Sisyphus. MacLennan sees in this ancient legend a perfect symbol for the puritan's compulsion to work – the sort of work represented in *Each Man's Son* by Daniel Ainslie's self-imposed task of learning Greek so that he can read Homer in the original. Daniel berates himself for his slow progress in Greek. When he finds that he has fallen behind in his self-imposed schedule, he accuses himself of stupidity. Margaret Ainslie, Daniel's wife, hates his huge Greek lexicon as a woman hates her husband's mistress. Furthermore, she notices that Daniel seems almost frightened when presented with the rare opportunity to rest and enjoy himself a little. When there is less work at the hospital, he makes more for himself at home.

Daniel's desire to master Greek represents something in his nature which his wife can neither reach nor understand. MacLennan on two separate occasions uses the verb "flog" in this connection. Daniel, unable to concentrate on Homer in the train on his way to a difficult surgery, blames himself for laziness, "and flogged himself on through another five lines." (*EMS* 118) Old Dr. MacKenzie, in the doctors' common room in the hospital, asks Daniel why he flogs himself to read Homer when he is tired. Earlier, Daniel had asked his wife, "What is there to do but work?" Dr. MacKenzie refuses to accept the idea that it is necessary for Daniel to work to the point of exhaustion. Not only his study of Greek but much of his medical work is unnecessary. Dr. MacKenzie tells Daniel that when he stops feeling sorry for himself he will make the brawling miners realize that he should not be bothered for trifles.

In the doctors' common room, Daniel tries to rest between operations, but finds himself stiff with a tension that has become chronic. Dr. MacKenzie tells Daniel that his tension is not caused by his work but is rather a new thing called hypertension, and Daniel is "rather a new type of man." It is not natural to court unnecessary work as Daniel has been doing. Dr. MacKenzie tells Daniel that he is trying to substitute work for life: that is, for a proper relationship with his wife, and a natural enjoyment of the beauty of the world. Daniel Ainslie has not always been this way. As a boy, he spent summers earning money before the mast, and he can still remember the smell of the forests wafting across the sea, the pungent scent of pine and balsam. He remembers the Margaree Valley, fragrant and beautiful, and the joy of fishing in the dawn: "Those had been good days."

Despite MacLennan's attack on Daniel Ainslie's misguided attempt at salvation through work, there is a definite reverence for work in this novel as in his earlier ones. There is also a mystical treatment of the doctor as an almost supernatural healer. *The Watch That Ends the Night* presents the same mystical treatment of the doctor in the figure of Jerome Martell. In *Each Man's Son*, Alan MacNeil, the boy whom Ainslie comes to seek as a possible son, thinks of Ainslie as "hardly a man at all. He was The Doctor, far above everyone else he knew." (*EMS* 51) The context here is ironical, suggesting that Ainslie's pride needs to be deflated. This idea is picked up in Dr. MacKenzie's challenge to Daniel to admit, at least occasionally, that he is only human.

But although pride is shown to be part of Ainslie's problem, and although he finds that he must "die" to this pride before he can find happiness, there are two sides to this coin. Daniel, as his old friend Dr. Doucette points out, may be a stuffed shirt but he is a lovely surgeon. It is as a surgeon that he has MacLennan's admiration and as a doctor that he represents MacLennan's ambivalent attitude towards work. Margaret Ainslie respected Daniel's home surgery, for she knows the high quality of the work done in it: "If it were not for his work, she thought, he would be intolerable. He was one of those rare doctors who invariably seem able to take a patient's ills upon themselves. She knew this and she reverenced the devotion which made him exhaust himself." (*EMS* 35) Because of Daniel's growing irritability and their frequent quarrels, she would find him intolerable *but for* his work. Here is a strange twist, for much of the novel is devoted to showing that it is just his compulsion to work which makes him intolerable. Margaret's reverence for the rare quality of her husband's work has come from her understanding that when he paces the floor, night after night, he is doing more than just pondering a case: "He was trying to *be* his patient, to find a way to convince him that he would not die." (*EMS* 35)

Daniel is intolerant of his wife's family, terming them lazy, too easy-going. As in MacLennan's earlier novels, there is a clash of values between puritan and non-puritan characters. Daniel feels that Mrs. Eldridge "stood for a state of mind opposed to everything his own emotions honoured." (*EMS* 45) But once again the surface simplicity dissolves into ambivalence. In the early chapters, Margaret seems to side with her family and their easy-going attitudes against her husband's obsession with work. Later, filled with pride in Dan's work, she condemns herself and her family for not having worried or struggled, for not having suffered, whereas Daniel has struggled from the day he was born. She feels painfully useless by comparison: "Her own world was too neat, too small and secure. His was the world of the sick and frightened." (*EMS* 160)

She thinks of the many lives he has saved, of the patients who would have died under other doctors, and of the price which Daniel has paid, without complaint, in order to do this. The hospital, as Dr. Ainslie tells the injured Newfoundland boy, is the best and safest place in the world, and in his hospital world Ainslie's skill has made him master. The boy's hands have been badly smashed in an accident, and Ainslie is represented by MacLennan as absorbing and conquering the boy's fear. Later, when the boy is hysterical at the loss of his hands, Ainslie calms and encourages him once more, assuring him that the remaining fingers on his right hand will hold a pencil, and that an education will enable him to earn his own living. MacLennan repeatedly emphasizes that the doctor's effort is "beyond the reach of words," (*EMS* 53) and that he somehow "merged himself with the patient." (*EMS* 75) As he hurries to the hospital when Alan is sick, Ainslie thinks that the doctor's task is "to go into the dark and share the patient's fear . . . to become everyone in order to be a doctor. Osler . . . woofing like a bear in order to give a child the curiosity which turned into the germ of a will to live. Was it sentimental?" (*EMS* 165) Definitely not. Mac-Lennan intends us to find this "a form of holiness" (his description of the work of Ainslie and Doucette as they perform delicate brain surgery on the injured longshoreman in Louisburg). We see, then, that when Daniel is with a patient, he becomes "totally the doctor." Gone is the puritan, burdened with an ancient curse, who needs to be cleansed of implanted fears. Gone is the suggestion that work is the senseless and unending labour of Sisyphus. MacLennan offers, instead, a mystical celebration of the doctor's work as a form of holiness.

Although *Each Man's Son* contains a reverence for work and for the doctor's mystic healing powers, this is not presented as the solution for the human tragedy. MacLennan's solution, in this novel, is love: love of one human individual for another, in the Christian sense of *agape*. We will find that MacLennan's affirmation differs from this in his fifth novel, *The Watch That Ends the Night*. In *Each Man's Son*, old Dr. MacKenzie understands man's need for love and acceptance, but Daniel Ainslie must learn it for himself and must suffer before he is able to do so. He suffers the death of his attitudes of guilt and pride. His story illustrates the quotation from the New Testament which serves as MacLennan's motto to the original edition: "Except a corn of wheat fall into the ground and die, it abideth alone: but if it die, it bringeth forth much fruit. . . ."

Ainslie, on his way to perform a brain surgery, accidentally meets Mollie MacNeil and her eight-year-old son Alan on the train to Louisburg. Mollie is taking an outing to help her get through the day while her husband Archie is fighting in Trenton, New Jersey. Ainslie is immediately attracted to the boy, feeling that no one has ever looked at him with such an unquestioning welcome as does Alan. For years, Ainslie has been longing for a son. It occurs to him that it would be a crime for such a boy, sensitive and intelligent, to go into the pits. It is Ainslie's plain duty to save Alan from this fate and give the boy a chance. Ainslie's spirits rise at the prospect. He feels that he could do anything if he had such a son. Because of this chance meeting, Ainslie performs exceptionally well in the delicate brain surgery done in the patient's home. After the operation, which he is sure will prove successful, Ainslie is filled with peaceful excitement, "for today he had fulfilled himself and justified himself, and he knew it." (*EMS* 122)

Ainslie aspires to save Alan from the mines. MacLennan shows us that Ainslie will be unable to save anyone until he himself has been saved from guilt and pride. Daniel has been shown as being hyper-critical of the work of both others and himself. His wife puts a loving interpretation on this habit. She explains his criticism as being really representative of a deep humility; his standards are so high that achievement will always fall short of them. She fails to see that this is a form of pride, not humility, in Daniel, for he is the criticizer as well as the criticized, the final judge of standards as well as the one who falls short of those standards: "It's the weakness in myself I can't forgive. . . . I suppose it's a tendency I inherited from my mother." (*EMS* 174) He tells Dr. MacKenzie of the hard years which the members of his family had suffered before his mother died. For several years after their barn had burned, they had been short of food, and before they were financially stable again their mother had died of pernicious anaemia. Daniel's father had refused to borrow money during this period, because he felt that this would have been mortgaging the future education of his sons.

Daniel interprets the actions of his father as strong and those of his mother as weak. His father had been afraid that the boys would be weak like their mother and had often warned Daniel against this. Fortunately for Daniel, old Dr. MacKenzie is familiar with his mother's case. He had known the family and attended Daniel's mother in her last illness. He tells Daniel that his mother had deprived herself of food in order to feed her sons, and this deprivation had led to her death. Thus Daniel owes his present health to his mother, and Dr. Dougald shows him how ironic it is to consider her weak, or lacking in will power: "You would do well to honour your father less and your mother more. She was a very loving woman." (*EMS* 176) MacLennan shows us a pattern repeating itself, the sins of the fathers being repeated by the children. As Ainslie's father had denied his mother, so Ainslie was trying to deny Alan's mother, to dismiss her as of no importance. Like his father, Daniel is unwilling to accept human frailty in himself or in others. We begin to see an ironic twist to Ainslie's fear that he has inherited weakness from his mother; he has indeed, but not in the sense he intended. He has inherited human nature, and his weakness lies in his pride, his determination to have his own will no matter what this may do to others, his need for love, and his stubborn refusal to give and accept love. (MacLennan's own view of man is thus curiously close to the Christian concept of original sin which he attacks.)

Archie MacNeil, the boxer, illustrates Ainslie's tragedy in another way. Both men typify suffering humanity, with Archie as the common man and Ainslie the uncommon, the intellectual. Archie has turned to professional fighting in an effort to escape the mines. He takes pride in his physical strength as Ainslie does in his medical skill. Like Ainslie, and like Stephen Lassiter near the end of *The Precipice*, Archie suffers the depths of loneliness. Unlike Ainslie and Lassiter, Archie has also suffered "in his flesh," as he intends to tell Mollie. We see him, finally, as a lost, bewildered man, alone in Montreal and then on a freight train heading for Cape Breton. Earlier, he has been deluded by his manager; now he is deluding himself. Half-blind, dizzy, slow, scarred and deformed, unable to sleep for pain, and suffering nightmares when he finally does slip into sleep, Archie heads for the peace and security which he hopes to find with Mollie. But he has already passed the point of no return, both physically and emotionally. Arriving home, he discovers the Frenchman Camire with his wife Mollie. In the violent fight which follows, Archie kills both Mollie and Camire. He is barely responsible for his actions, hardly conscious of what he has done. Ainslie, observing the profound disintegration occurring in Archie's entire body, addresses him with extreme gentleness.

Archie's conflict ends in tragedy, whereas for Dr. Ainslie there is a final triumph. But Ainslie has first to experience a kind of death. He learns that Mollie intends to marry Camire and take Alan away. Ainslie knows that he has lost the boy, and feels that he has driven Mollie to Camire. He feels engulfed by a terrible fatigue, a total spiritual exhaustion. Ainslie has been suffering under the ancient curse. Fear and guilt have made him afraid of love and life itself. MacLennan pours out his bitterness on "the men who invented the curse." He calls them criminals and blames them for generations of ruined lives: "The criminals slept well, and their names were sanctified." (*EMS* 201) Ainslie feels that he is now free from the curse, but free only to wander through an abyss of emptiness, a sinister landscape with neither god nor devil, "a world without purpose, without meaning, without intelligence." His rejection of the fears implanted by Calvinism is painted as a death of the spirit, a journey through purgatory and emptiness to his "core." We should recall the words of Dr. MacKenzie, that Ainslie really seeks a God, not a son.

Out of this purgatory and emptiness, Ainslie's rebirth begins, slowly at first, with a simple feeling of acceptance. He discovers that he is ready to go on with life. He accepts the beauty of the world, represented by the brook at his feet. He accepts, for the first time, his wife's love, the surest haven he has ever known. He accepts the anticipated loss of Alan, as he realizes that he should not and cannot deprive Mollie of her son. And he accepts his work, without the former loss of energy through nervous frustration. Ainslie has begun to realize that forgiveness cannot be earned, as Dr. MacKenzie told him earlier.

Mollie MacNeil's behaviour with regard to Camire fits into Mac-Lennan's general pattern of moral responsibility concerning sex. Mollie is no puritan, by MacLennan's definition. Her son Alan, secure in his mother's love, has never even heard of sin before he encounters Mrs. MacCuish. Mollie refuses to do anything of which Alan might be ashamed. She answers Camire's insistence that sexual relations are natural and necessary, when her husband has left her, by saying that they would not be, just then. Despite the surface resemblance of the Frenchman's argument to MacLennan's own attacks on puritanism, the author uses Mollie to suggest that self-denial is a necessary good. Her final surrender to Camire precipitates tragedy. The forces which are converging to a tragic climax cannot be stemmed. Archie returns home to find, not the peace and security he craves, but Camire and Mollie together. Alan is a horrified witness to the ensuing fight, "understanding none of it, yet feeling all of it, so that for the rest of his life all the violence of the world would be the violence of this night." It will take time for Margaret and Daniel Ainslie's love to heal his psychic scars.

Mollie's death acts redemptively for Daniel. It completes his rebirth which began by the brook after he first realized that he has harmed Mollie and will lose Alan. Ainslie now understands the evil of human pride and the extent of his own. Brokenly, he tells Dr. MacKenzie that he has killed Mollie as his father killed his mother: "Through arrogance, the both of us. Through total incapacity to understand that in comparison with a loving human being, everything else is worthless." The fact that Mollie's death is required to end Daniel's pride and arrogance provides an interesting analogy with the Christian doctrine of the atoning death of Christ. Daniel finally understands what Dr. MacKenzie has tried in vain to teach him earlier: the need and the allness of love.[4]

NOTES

1. The weaknesses in MacLennan's interpretation of Calvinism, and of Protestant Christianity in general, are discussed in Chapters One and Three.

2. Cf. Alec Lucas, *Hugh MacLennan*, Canadian Writers No. 8 (Toronto: McClelland and Stewart, 1970), p. 24: "Does he sterilize his wife because he unconsciously assumes he is betraying his mother or his stern father and his God through her and so strikes on a way to punish himself and his wife for enjoying sex?"

3. Cf. Robert H. Cockburn, *The Novels of Hugh MacLennan* (Montreal: Harvest House, 1969), p. 92: "In fact, the theme – the repression of love through a combination of guilt and pride – and the action, a quest for compassion and personal fulfillment, are superbly unified."

4. Ann Roberts, "The Dilemma of Hugh MacLennan," *Marxist Quarterly* (Autumn 1962), p. 63, objects to MacLennan's emphasis on personal love to the neglect of "coherent positive social action." Alec Lucas, *Hugh MacLennan*, p. 56, answers her objection, defending MacLennan's work for its insistence that social action be "based on the same elements that help constitute personal love; namely, tolerance, kindness, compassion, and benevolence – all qualities that have little place in a purely rational ethic."

7 'THE CORNY OLD VERITIES, TRUTH AND FUN'

The pursuit of truth by means of fun is Cohen's favourite game. Contemporary puritanism, as MacLennan emphasizes, need not necessarily be attached to any religion at all. And conversely, the values common to MacLennan and the historic Puritans – the ethical emphasis, the sense of spiritual dedication in one's work, and a profound respect for the intellect – are also strong in the Jewish tradition. We have seen how some of the ideals of the seventeenth-century reformers were corrupted into what MacLennan calls taboos and shibboleths. Cohen uses the Breavman family name as a symbol for the traditional ideals of his nation (both Jewish and Canadian), and proceeds to attack the present representatives of this tradition for having betrayed the ideal.

Lawrence Breavman, hero of *The Favorite Game*, provides the focus for this attack. As a child (most children are iconoclasts) and a developing artist, Breavman is the archetypal Outsider, the lonely seer. It is the romantic view of the artist as prophet, priest, magician; as Lucifer and Faust. We have a classic example of the type in Arthur Rimbaud's letter of May 15, 1871, to his friend Paul Demeny. Australian novelist Patrick White uses this romantic view in *The Vivisector* in order to satirize it.[1] The youthful James Joyce was tempted by this view of the artist, but he reveals its immaturity in his portrait of the artist *as a young man*. Is Cohen's romantic portrait of the artist "straight," or ironic? Both, surely. Cohen is a romanticist *and* a satirist, and his ambivalence comes through in his unusual style, at once lyric and Rabelaisian. As Michael Ondaatje notes, "unlike Stephen Daedelus, Breavman is quite aware of how ironic he is," and yet "Cohen is still the great romantic."[2]

Breavman discovers his vocation as artist between the ages of sixteen and twenty-one (Book II). His quest for freedom involves an answer to the problem of time, loss and decay. He sees that *time stops* in the art of Henri Rousseau. To capture this distance and stasis becomes his artistic objective. Only "that important second" of his beloved as frozen in art, not the everyday appearance, is important. Night drives with Krantz at high speed produce the same feeling of a reality superior to ordinary reality, an escape from time. In one luminous moment the speeding Breavman becomes conscious of his fate as an artist. It is an epiphany comparable to that of Joyce's Stephen, when the sight of a solitary girl by the sea calls him to the priesthood of art. Breavman knows he will experience beauty and despair, creative pain, humility and power. The stasis of art is the tenth of a second for which he has traded all the presidencies.

In one incident, Breavman's relation to Tamara is twice-distanced through a fiction which the fictional Breavman is writing. The scene parodies the self-conscious decadence of the nineties: "Tonight we are glorious and degraded, knighted and crushed, beautiful and disgusting. Sweat is perfume. Gasps are bells." (*FG* 77)[3] The lyricism is purposely undercut by remarks such as "Horseshit." The lover worries lest their sentimental hoaxing should lead to serious reflection, something he cannot face. His self-conscious nostalgia seems to cover an inner wound and parodies the unnaturally careful gestures of a Hemingway war casualty such as Nick, in "Big Two-Hearted River." The twice-fictionalized Breavman recognizes that the Pygmalion element in his feeling for Tamara is a creator's narcissistic love for his creation.

The paradoxical unity of the human body and spirit is an important aspect of the novel's theme, which centres in the seeming contradiction of the performance of art and the impermanence of life. The ironic conflict between artist and ordinary man, a conflict which must be sustained in one body, belongs to this theme. As a young boy, Breavman experiences a private apocalypse at the sight of the white body of the child Lisa. The scene is both lyric and comic, as the boy's awed wonder ("There were white flowers growing out of all her pores") contrasts with Lisa's no-nonsense attitude and Krantz' stolidity. Breavman and Lisa play the game of the Soldier and the Whore, both roles idealized: "They had no knowledge of the sordid aspect of brothels, and who knows if there is one?" (The *naïveté* presumably belongs to Breavman, not Cohen.)

The young adolescents are preoccupied with "games of flesh, love, curiosity." Breavman and Lisa strike gold in the maid's room, in the form of a hand-viewed film which demonstrates, with frank and beguiling simplicity, the facts and figures of physical love. The multiracial character of the filmed couples, "all without their national costumes on," is termed a blow for World Federalism. Cohen's comic technique frequently uses indirection to reveal the impact of an event on the hero's consciousness. The boy's reaction to the maid's film is: if this is the way things are, then why is anybody working?

The last episode in Book I, the end of Breavman's childhood, shows him employing the technique learned from pulp-paper manuals to hypnotize Heather, the maid. Once hypnotized, Breavman directs her to remove her clothes. "Astonished, happy, and frightened" by the sight of her body, he has an orgasm by masturbating. A morally dubious situation? In theory, yes. But in the fictional episode, Cohen's comic technique distances and controls the moral judgement. The mood is at once lyric, comic, earthy. The youth is awed both by the magical power of hypnosis (a metaphor for art) and by the beauty of the girl's body. He stares like Cortés over his new ocean. Awe turns to terror as he wonders whether he has driven the girl insane, and struggles to bring her out of the trance. Heather is unconcerned by the discovery of her panties, forgotten behind the couch: " 'Jewish people.' She sighed. 'Education!' " She eventually runs off with a soldier, and Breavman mourns her loss thus: "Where are you Heather . . . ? I might have gone straight. Poemless, a baron of industry."

The artist as Outsider stands in judgement over the Insiders, the conventional ones, the social conformists. It is essentially a moral stance, that of the immoral moralist. Breavman is frequently depicted as more moral than the elders who would condemn many of his actions. And Breavman's growth towards maturity (for this is a *kunstleroman*, a novel of the education of the artist-hero) is a spiritual odyssey, a growth in compassion and human understanding. The novel's four books deal with four stages in the life of Lawrence Breavman: childhood; adolescence; early maturity; and suffering, loss, guilt. It is an odyssey where sex is depicted as the basis for the embryonic artist's acquisition of knowledge and interpretation of experience.

Breavman, like Joyce's Stephen, sees himself as the conscience of his race. To the current Montreal joke, that the Jews are the conscience of the world and the Breavmans are the conscience of the Jews, Lawrence Breavman adds a corollary; he is the conscience of the Breavmans, one of the loyal remnant, "super-Christians." It is suspected that the Breavmans are currently in a decline and may begin to "speak with accents." The parody of the traditional British fear of native or Cockney accents corrupting the pure Oxonian tones carries a double entendre: the adult community has become morally degenerate. As adolescents, Breavman and his friend Krantz warm to the attack:

> Weren't they supposed to be a holy people consecrated to purity, service, spiritual honesty? Weren't they a nation set apart?
> Why had the idea of a jealously guarded sanctity degenerated into a sly contempt for the goy, empty of self-criticism?
> Parents were traitors. . . .
> Smug traitors who believed spiritual fulfillment had been achieved because Einstein and Heifetz are Jews. (*FG* 38)

The adolescent Krantz and Breavman, like the kids in Shebib's film "Rip-Off," know more about what they don't want than about what they do.

The Breavman name is an ambivalent symbol. On the one hand it is identified with the artist as the conscience of his race. On the other, it suggests the Victorian ideals honoured by his parents' generation. It is in the latter sense that Lawrence's father is described as being mercilessly opposed to all that is "weak, taboo, *unBreavmanlike* [italics mine]." (*FG* 24) To be a Breavman in this sense is to adhere to the late-nineteenth- and early-twentieth-century trust in reason and in the "civilized" gentleman's humanitarian code of ethics. Lawrence's father wears English-type suits, the very fabric saturated with English reticence. His face "glows with Victorian reason and decency." (With reference to "decent," I think of the many times I heard the word pronounced by my English mother as a moral judgement.) Cohen's use of the word "Victorian" is very similar to MacLennan's, in *Return of the Sphinx*, where Alan Ainslie believes that his Victorian heritage has died, and part of himself with it.

The Breavman ethic begins: "We are Victorian gentlemen of Hebraic persuasion." Deftly, in a few short paragraphs, Lawrence's father is developed as the archetypal Victorian. He is strongly attracted to science and machinery, and awed by a burgeoning technology. The click of his gun, to the child's ears, is "the marvellous sound of all murderous scientific achievement." The pages of the poetry books given him at his bar mitzvah are left uncut. He presses "How To" books upon his son, who hates them increasingly as his father lies dying. The child tears at the careful diagrams, "to scorn the world of detail, information, precision, all the false knowledge which cannot intrude on decay." Yet the boy, Lawrence, unlike his parents, is not afraid of death (or life) and would have had the father's coffin left open longer.

Despite the uncut poetry pages, Breavman's father is "double-natured," and the boy understands and loves this ambivalence, for it is part of his own experience. Privately, he sees his father as "the persecuted brother, the near-poet, the innocent of the machine toys, the sighing judge who listens but does not sentence. . . . He can rest. *Breavman has inherited all his concerns* [italics mine]." (*FG* 24) The Breavman name is thus identified with a code of values, a betrayal or distortion of those values, and a criticism of that betrayal. George Robertson suggests that "loss is love's counter-theme, Breavman's name presumably a pun on bereavement."[4] There are other connotations: *brief-man* suggests man's participation in time and decay (including moral corruption), a brevity which the novel contrasts with the stasis of art. Hence the idea that the artist is the conscience of his race implies an ideal standpoint or vision outside the moral and temporal flux.

In the novel's fourth book, Cohen's criticism of contemporary Canadian society is channelled mainly through Breavman's attitude towards the twelve-year-old Martin Stark and his mother.[5] Whereas others see the mathematical Martin as half-nut, half-genius, Breavman sees him as "that rarest creature, a blissful mad-child," "a divine idiot." Shades of Dostoevski. The divine fool has a long tradition in Western literature (Bunyan's Mr. Feeble-minded is one example) and is essentially a romantic conception. Breavman's *rapport* with the child is based on an appreciation of his madness as freedom. He tells Krantz that the child is the only free person he has met, and that his actions are therefore uniquely important. Krantz, rejecting this interpretation, sides with Mrs. Stark, who wants her child to be forced into the acceptable social mold, "integrated, inconspicuous." The confrontation over Martin marks the end of Krantz' and Breavman's friendship, and is a last "true meeting" separating the revolutionary artist-Outsider from his conforming friend. Krantz defects to society-as-it-is. Breavman holds out for society-as-it-should-be, City of God.

Martin, fulfilling his mosquito-killing mission, is run over by a tractor in the marsh. His funeral is the occasion for a bitter attack on religious hypocrisy and materialism:

A religious stink hovers above this city and we all breathe it. . . . A religious stink composed of musty shrine and tabernacle smells, decayed wreaths and rotting bar-mitzvah tables. Boredom, money, vanity, guilt packs the pews.

The candles, memorials, eternal lights shine unconvincingly, like neon signs, sincere as advertising. . . . Good lovers turn away. *(FG* 184)

Cohen charges that the sanctuary of the sixties, whether Christian or Jewish, is a temple to Mammon from which "good lovers," or the sincerely religious, turn away. A valid attack? It is a partial truth, obviously not the complete truth, about the state of Church and Synagogue in Canada today. "Good lovers" welcome criticism as a cleansing force.

Evelyn Waugh's *The Loved One* is a macabre and wonderfully funny satire on contemporary funeral customs. But Martin's funeral is one of the rare occasions when Cohen has nothing funny to say. The funeral chapel, with its artificial hush and its air conditioning, is irrelevant to the child's real death, and conspires against the expression of the family's grief. The death and the funeral, together, have destroyed the prosaic, "comfortable" world.

One of the funniest pieces of social criticism (Book I, 23) is in connection with a dance in Breavman's early adolescence. Ashamed of his smallness, he thinks of himself as The Cunning Dwarf, and adds height by packing Kleenex into the soles of his shoes. Apparent success ("Science triumphs again") gives way, as the evening wears on, to physical agony. Hell is envisaged as an eternal Bunny Hop with sore feet. Since it is rumoured that one of the girls stuffs her bra with paper tissues, Kleenex becomes the metaphor for hypocrisy, deception and the imitations so prevalent in our culture. Cohen uses hyperbole and incremental repetition effectively. Breavman thinks that perhaps everyone there is wearing a Kleenex prop: "Maybe some had Kleenex noses and Kleenex ears and Kleenex hands. Depression seized him." The metaphor recurs from time to time. The ideal girls sought by Breavman and his bosom friend Krantz are "not Kleenex girls." The *reductio ad absurdum*, in a hypothetical chain of murders by drowning, is a moist Kleenex. In opposition to the Kleenex world are natural items which Breavman admires, such as the park gardeners' brooms made of real branches.

Breavman rejects the puritan work ethic of the Insider community. Their code requires the individual to work at a regular job, and to judge success in terms of climbing the job ladder. (Cohen's second novel, playing on failure as an ironic concept, satirized the attempt to plan one's life in these terms. The narrator finds himself "fooled" by his briefcase, "led astray" by tidy notes into the illusion of importance and success. He starts "making plans like a graduating class.") Breavman will have none of it, and some of the novel's funniest scenes revolve around this rebellion. His mother takes it as a personal injury that her adolescent son is "wasting" his life in bed during the daytime, and rejecting the pattern of three square meals a day. She calls him "a traitor not a son" – a traitor to her generation's code. Her stage-managed hysteria, as she offers him a long list of foods, is marvellously comic. His mother uses material things (food, first, and household goods, later) as a weapon of control, a bribe for adopting her life-style, a demand for gratitude and subservience. Her self-pity and self-hatred make a powerful portrait of guilt and fear. There is guilt, and a strange compulsive element in her ostensible thankfulness for the food which they have in abundance: "who's going to drink all the wine, that's a shame, Lawrence, look at them, feel the weight of this grapefruit, we're so lucky, and meat, three kinds. . . ."

The adolescent boy, however, has his own version of work. He roams the park at night, looking, feeling, reflecting, mythologizing his own life and that of others – preparing for his vocation as artist. The park is the green heart which affords bravery, beauty, power; and poetry, the best part of everyone's life. The aspiring artist is already the rebel, the beautiful loser, the Outsider: "He hated the men floating in sleep in the big stone houses. Because their lives were ordered and their rooms tidy. Because they got up every morning and did their public work. Because they weren't going to dynamite their factories and have naked parties in the fire." (*FG* 59)

Breavman does a brief stint in a brass foundry, for penance. His mother is embarrassed when people ask her about her son and she must reluctantly confess he is a factory worker. He has, unlike the solid citizen, no plans for the future, and parodies those who do, turning their ordered lives into a game of Monopoly: "It's all over. Go back to your homes. Do not pass Go. Do not collect two hundred dollars. . . . Can't you see it's all done with?"

This pattern prepares us for Breavman's attitude towards Martin, another Outsider. No one but Breavman appreciates the beauty of Martin's character, and sees the self-fulfilment and happiness which the child is capable of when left to his own mathematical devices. Martin, and those who would alter him, provide the context for Breavman's connection between storm troopers, bands of crusaders, gangs of slaves and righteous citizens who insist that everyone be integrated and inconspicuous conformists.

Breavman's love for Shell becomes a strong temptation to "join the world" and "be a citizen with a woman and a job." His struggle with this temptation (Book III) is depicted as a struggle between himself as Artist and his deputy or double, the lover of Shell. He is fully aware of the irony involved in his rejection of her.[6] He sees his artist self as the lover or celebrant of all living things, and of life itself. He believes he can create only in lonely freedom, and that he must shun the comfort of married love, lest it put the "Breavman eye" to sleep. The artist's eye is something "which could apply her beauty to streets, traffic, mountains, ignite the landscape." Love, separation and a mysterious failure of commitment, as with Shell, are also frequent themes in Cohen's songs.

Canada, like the Breavman name, is an ambivalent concept. Occasionally, the Canadian nation becomes an apocalyptic metaphor for the artist's dream of an ideal community. Breavman, on the beach with Norma, thinks: "America was lost, the scabs ruled everything, the skyscrapers of chrome would never budge, but Canada was here, infant dream, the stars high and sharp and cold, and the enemies were brittle and easy and English." (*FG* 64) In an interview with Michael Harris, Cohen said: "But I do love Canada, just because it isn't America and I have, I suppose, foolish dreams about Canada. I believe it could somehow avoid American mistakes, and it could really be *that* country that becomes a noble country, not a powerful country."[7]

A more frequent pattern, however, connects Canada with the Insiders: philistine, bourgeois, conventional, stodgy. Conformists all. Breavman (like F., in *Beautiful Losers*) sees the Insiders as betrayers of the ideal, who pay lip service to their spiritual heritage. As an adult, he rejoices that he was trained in childhood to suspect his Gentile neighbours. He can now extend this criticism to his own "tribe." Thus the Jewish experience of being an Outsider becomes Breavman's own personal experience, as the non-conforming artist criticizes the tribal society of the nation as a whole: "Hello Canada, you big Canada, you dull, beautiful resources. Everybody is Canadian. The Jew's disguise won't work." (*FG* 180) The disguise no longer holds because, Cohen charges, Canada is a conforming society where no one is allowed to be different.

Earlier, Breavman satirizes the prevailing theory of Canada as a mosaic of different nationalities, rather than a "melting pot," the American pattern: "That's why we're great, Krantz. The cross-fertilization." In Cohen's ironic comedy, it is a cross-fertilization of defects, not strengths, where the French and the Jews are "vicious" and the English-Canadians "absurd." The mosaic theory affords an explanation as to why Canadians have been especially conscious of history. The narrator thinks of all Canadians as immigrants whose past, like that of the Canadian nation, happened somewhere else:

"Each man speaks with his father's tongue. Just as there are no Canadians, there are no Montrealers. Ask a man who he is and he names a race." (*FG* 102) An extreme view, surely. But then hyperbole is one of Cohen's tools. The mosaic of cultural patterns can (and has, to some extent) become the basis for a new pluralistic unity in the Canadian nation.[8] And despite the burden of our colonial mentality, our national past has happened *here* for several hundred years, not just "somewhere else."

Breavman sees Canadian society as a cultural desert, a nation "desperate for a Keats," where writers are interviewed on TV for the sole purpose of giving the rest of the nation a good laugh. "Do they have Art in Winnipeg?" he inquires at a cocktail party. In *Two Solitudes*, Dennis Morey describes his home town of Winnipeg in a similar fashion, as puritan and beauty-hating. (In 1945, the Winnipeg Ballet Company was yet to come.) Cohen's crack probably reflects the idea that eastern Canada is the locus of such artistic culture as we have. The concept is shockingly outdated by the late sixties. But he puts his finger most amusingly on the intellectual element in our puritan heritage: "Literary meetings are the manner in which Anglophiles express passion." English Montreal is described in *Beautiful Losers* as an "obscure mental factory."

In his chosen role as Artist, Breavman frequently undercuts his own pose. He admits that his disciplined melancholy is a hoax, "a calculated display of suffering" to advance himself personally. Seeing that upper-class Gentiles in Montreal are "pledged to Culture (like all good Canadians)," Breavman becomes "a kind of mild Dylan Thomas, talent and behavior modified for Canadian tastes." He blames the barren philistine nature of the culture for forcing him into these unnatural poses.

Sex provides a focus for the artist's iconoclastic tendencies and for his conflict with a narrowly-interpreted puritan tradition in Canada. Breavman rationalizes his desires to sleep with the married Lisa, his childhood love: "It was a free country. The old taboos were in disrepute. They were grown up and wouldn't be called in for supper. . . . Breavman, thou false lech, your room hideously empty as your charity smile." (*FG* 100) He is plainly on the defensive. Lisa has come to him primarily for revenge upon the husband who has betrayed her. Breavman and Lisa's love-making is termed "a protest against luck and circumstance," and Breavman's strongest emotion is a poignant sense of wonder and loss concerning *Lisa the child*, with whom he will never sleep.

Cohen's sexual ethic is not simply licence, as will be seen in our analysis of *Beautiful Losers*. A belief in the unity of the human body and spirit underlies both novels. In *The Favorite Game*, there is mild disdain for Med, the Expert Fool. The handsome young Lebanese professor has chosen academic life because of the opportunities for casual love affairs which he expects it to provide. (Obviously his original expectations were formed in Lebanon or America, rather than in the puritan halls of Canadian campuses.) He prides himself on the perfection of his love-making *technique* and is dedicated to this, his real profession. Both Breavman and Shell see him as a clown, whose phoniness can only amuse.

The hypocrisy of Shell's husband with regard to sex is treated quite differently from Med's clowning. Gordon's desire for sex stops with self-gratification; thus Shell, before her affair with Breavman, is all of D.H. Lawrence's frustrated virgins rolled into one. Cohen depicts the result of her frustration as an unnatural separation of body and spirit, with loving sexual relations as the key to integration and peace: "Desire made her close her eyes, not for Gordon, not for a prince, but for the human man who would return her to her envelope of skin and sit beside her in the afternoon light." (*FG* 122) After sexual relations with Med, she succumbs to a wave of unfocused hatred, not for the "too simple" Med, but for Gordon and for her own "silly body." Without passion, she is merely a tenant in a body *not her own*.

There is a remarkable poignancy and fragility in many of the Shell episodes. Breavman initially sees her as a twentieth-century surrealist version of Botticelli's archetypal beauty rising from the waves: "Not Botticelli – Giacometti." Shell's father covers his sexual failure by an amiable patience towards his wife and affectionate kisses before and after meals. Gordon is the Chatterley archetype of impotence (without, in Gordon's case, the excuse of a war wound). The apparently well-ordered existence of Gordon's marriage to Shell is in reality a ruin which is making her ill. The fleshless, elongated and gloomy figures of Alberto Giacometti suggest her plight. She thinks of sex as the doorway to sanity and rest.

The novel pictures the failure of Gordon and of Shell's father as part of the general masculine failure of American society. A cocktail toast is dedicated to the extinct American male. The list of men lost to analysts and psychological Westerns includes gamekeepers, but this Lawrencian parody is in earnest, for all its fun. Cohen's two novels contain repeated attacks on the greed and materialism of our advertising culture. *Why* the ever-changing fashions, he asks, why the opulent fabrics, the coiffures, cosmetics and clever decor?

"Whom to delight? . . . The beginning was wrong. The coupling did not occur." The facade of sexuality covers a nothingness. Shell thinks that elegance and grace should evolve from "a sweet struggle of the flesh. Otherwise it was puppetry, hideous. She began to understand peace as an aftermath." (*FG* 121) It becomes Breavman's ambition to give Shell back her body, to make her feel herself whole. He plays Pygmalion, as he has done with Tamara. But whereas he has loved only what Tamara represented, he learns to love Shell as an individual, a particular person with whom he has "collided."

The Favorite Game is concerned with love and loss, as one critic notes, but Cohen centres both these experiences in the unity of the body and spirit. Through loving Shell, Breavman discovers that the beauty of the flesh is "just the soul's everyday clothes." But life in the flesh involves dying, and the child understands that he is part of a mysterious passage of time and pattern of growth which is leading not only to maturity but to decay and death: "A scar is what happens when *the word is made flesh* [italics mine]." (*FG* 9) His mother mourns the loss of the "real face" of her youth; the body of Breavman's dead rat fertilizes the pansies: and the aged father's swollen body has somehow replaced the strong firm body which once waded up rivers in rubber boots. Hence the child who is to become an artist tears at the scientific books recommended by his dying father, sensing that science is as helpless as he is, ultimately, to prevent aging and death. As an adult, Breavman knows that it is not simply that things decay. The things themselves *are* decay, "the monuments were *made* of worms."[9] *Death is the body's final scar.* The fourth books celebrates "the bodies Breavman lost." They are bodies he has loved, killed, hurt, deserted; bodies he has preserved whole and perfect in art. The latter, he fears, is a kind of permanence which is "no comfort to anyone."

During childhood and adolescence, before Krantz defects to the Insiders, the two friends take turns being straight man for one another's jests. They are "two Talmudists, delighting in their dialectic which was a disguise for love." They are two Davids, aiming their slings at a Kleenex world which they reject. And their ammunition for the battle? *Fun.* Truly a slingshot weapon against Madison Avenue and the Bomb. Cohen's art is an expression of what he calls "the corny old verities, truth and fun." (*FG* 37) His incorrigible, irrepressible technique is one with everything he has to tell us. Like Bernard Kops, he shows us the truth of the Talmud saying, "the world is a wedding."

NOTES

1. See *Rimbaud: Complete Works, Selected Letters,* ed. W. Fowlie (Chicago: 1966), p. 307, for Rimbaud's description of the artist-seer; and Patricia A. Morley, "Doppelganger's Dilemma: Artist and Man in *The Vivisector,*" *Queen's Quarterly,* 78 (Autumn 1971), 407, and *passim,* for White's treatment of the same subject.

2. Michael Ondaatje, *Leonard Cohen,* Canadian Writers 5 (Toronto: McClelland and Stewart, 1970), pp. 24, 44.

3. Cf. Sandra Djwa, "Leonard Cohen. Black Romantic," *Canadian Literature,* 34 (1967), 32-42. Djwa slights the ironic self-consciousness which surrounds Cohen's "satanism" or decadence, and places him in the *fin de siècle* tradition of Baudelaire and Gênet.

4. George Robertson, "Love and Loss," *Canadian Literature,* 19 (1964), 69.

5. Robertson, "Love and Loss," p. 70, finds the whole Martin episode "uniquely unconvincing," and argues that Breavman's protectiveness here is out of character since he has acted irresponsibly in earlier adult encounters. This ignores Breavman's *growth* towards maturity, as shown, for example, in the difference in Breavman's relationship with Tamara and with Shell.

6. Ondaatje, *Leonard Cohen,* p. 32, describes the breakdown of his relationship with Shell as "the archetypal one in all of Cohen's writing."

7. Michael Harris, "Leonard Cohen: The Poet as Hero. 2," *Saturday Night* (June 1969), p. 28.

8. See Stuart E. Rosenberg, *The Jewish Community in Canada. In the Midst of Freedom,* Vol. 2 (Toronto: McClelland and Stewart, 1971), 203: "If the Jewish community is to attract the best spirits among the new generation it will have to become more than just another ethnic group within the context of the 'Canadian mosaic.' "

9. Cf. Patrick White's treatment of *Dreck* or dirt in *The Vivisector,* discussed in Patricia A. Morley, "Doppelganger's Dilemma: Artist and Man in *The Vivisector,*" and in *The Mystery of Unity: Theme and Technique in the Novels of Patrick White* (Montreal: McGill-Queen's University Press, 1972), Chapter 11. See also my article on *The Favorite Game,* " 'The knowledge of strangerhood': 'The monuments were *made* of worms,' " *Journal of Canadian Fiction,* 3 (August 1972).

8 'IS MATTER HOLY?'

Cohen's mystical attitude towards matter and the human body is relevant to our examination of changing Canadian mores because the kind of puritanism which MacLennan attacks directly, and Cohen indirectly, has downgraded the body in favour of the spirit. Cohen refuses to accept their separation. Victorian niceties combined with puritan asceticism to establish the myth of the clean and socially acceptable body, all messy functions out of sight, out of mind, and certainly out of literature. Cohen's generation set out to rediscover the body, and Cohen depicts time and life itself as one vast orgasm, "the cunt of now, soak of the present." (*BL* 206)

I have suggested earlier that the initial reading of *Beautiful Losers* might subject the average Canadian to cultural shock. The advance in sexual frankness between, say, D.H. Lawrence's *Lady Chatterley's Lover* and *Beautiful Losers* would leave a small-town librarian or member of the P.T.A. gasping for breath. And the sexual frankness is central, not peripheral. The human body is the focus for the novel because Cohen believes it to be the basis of our human experience. I question Don Owen's application of "Eastern" to the idea that the erotic is at the very core of the spiritual, since many types of Buddhism are extremely ascetic, puritanical by MacLennan's definition. I would agree, however, with his assessment that "It takes a great deal of courage to confront the sexual fear that separates us all. In part, it's this sexual courage that makes Leonard so popular with the kids, who make fewer distinctions in sexual matters than we do."[1]

The body is both funny and beautiful, like the rest of creation. The intricate teacher-pupil relationship between F. and the narrator of Book One is designed to lead the narrator, and the reader, towards this understanding. The narrator is lonely; the narrator is constipated. The two conditions are two faces of the same coin; constipation becomes a metaphor for isolation. Shitless, the narrator sees himself as the *dead* centre of a universe which is a closed system, devoid of possibilities. No exit. "This is the brutal solitude of constipation, this is the way the world is lost." (*BL* 40) He craves relationship or interchange with the rest of creation ("I don't want to live inside!"), and tries to bribe God, with the cunning frenzy born of desperation: "My portion of the world's work will not be done, I warn you." Like James Joyce and Samuel Beckett, Cohen can make superb comedy out of metaphysics. The recurrent motif of constipation also suggests that the novel may serve the reader as a laxative with which to purge himself of a hypocritical shame of the body, a shame which degrades and destroys what it pretends to revere. But Cohen's iconoclasm is creative rather than destructive, and *Beautiful Losers* is certainly not part of what Robert Fulford terms "the literature of exhaustion."[2]

The chief characters in both *Beautiful Losers* and MacLennan's *Return of the Sphinx* are orphans, another variant on the theme of isolation. F. begins the long letter, which serves as Book Two of *Beautiful Losers,* by calling his friend his favourite male orphan. The wart removal takes place in the orphanage where F. and his friend are together as boys. F.'s friend, dreaming of leadership and glory, while experiencing only pain and humiliation, describes himself as loving society "as only an orphan can."

F. has advised his friend to make love to a saint. This ideal human being is defined as "someone who has achieved a remote human possibility," (*BL* 95) a focus of loving energy who introduces balance into the chaos of existence. The saint does not eliminate chaos, but rides it "like an escaped ski," an image used several times in *The Favorite Game.* In this passage in *Beautiful Losers,* Cohen's narrator pictures the saint as one who loves and is at home in the world, rather than longing to escape from it to God. "But why fuck one?" By way of explanation, the narrator describes a unique and blessed experience with his wife the first time they made love: "for a blessed second truly I was not alone, I was part of a family. . . . Is that what you will cause me to feel, Catherine Tekakwitha?" (*BL* 96)

Catherine is the subject of the narrator's historical research and his spiritual quest. The Iroquois Virgin has been dead some 300 years. Now virginity is scarcely Cohen's ideal. But neither was it the ideal of her own century, of her tribe or of the French Roman Catholic community. Everybody, Christian and heathen alike, attempted to force Catherine to marry. This leads F. to conclude that every community is by nature ultimately secular. In both novels Cohen attacks the tyranny of the majority and defends the freedom of the individual to be different, to explore the remote human possibilities, and to defy the conformity which society attempts to enforce.

"Is matter holy?" (*BL* 6) The narrator of *Beautiful Losers* poses the question, and both of Cohen's novels answer "yes." The wonder of life, and the unity of flesh and spirit, are themes in Cohen's novels as in his poetry. Cohen's vision is similar to that which underlies Yeats' great line, "Fair and foul are near of kin." In *Beautiful Losers*, the scattered references to the holiness of fair and foul alike make a coherent pattern. Moreover, the entire technique, where much of the humour is based upon flamboyant and gross sexuality and delightful crudities, is designed to shock us into admitting that bodily functions are no cause for shame.

In Book One, the narrator wryly recognizes F.'s profundity in choosing to make love to ugly women. As F. puts it, who is he to refuse the universe? F. tries in vain to convince the narrator that the world is *all diamond*, "the shit glory tree" (*BL* 12), *not* diamonds of good nestling in shit: "He kept to his diamond line. Catherine Tekakwitha, I wanted to believe him." F. is a student of the cabala, the body of Jewish writings which expound the mystical oneness of all things. The narrator has a vision, "a beautiful knowledge of unity," where all the disparates of the world are strung together to form a necklace "of incomparable beauty and unmeaning." (*BL* 17) But this is not the same as a fake universal, and F. warns: connect nothing. Cabalistic connections, he implies, are only for the philosophically mature, or those over seventy. We must first understand that people are different, roses are different, and the philosopher as well as the artist cherishes these particularities.

"Even The World Has A Body," the narrator records one morning. He pays homage to the Jesuits for conquering the frontier between the natural and the supernatural, for compelling men to acknowledge that the earth is a province of eternity, for knowing "that lameness is only an aspect of perfection, just as weeds are flowers which no one collects." (*BL* 100) God is the "shit-enhaloed Accuser of the World," and the lavatory, a thrilling temple of the Profane. Will anyone believe him? The narrator sadly concludes that, in line with his pattern of failure, he has succeeded only in offending everyone. The attack in *The Favorite Game* upon Shell's husband, Gordon, for destroying his wife with his sexlessness, and Breavman's dedication to making her whole, can now be seen as part of a coherent sexual ethic. Sex has always been the favourite topic for comedians, so Cohen works in a time-honoured tradition. His "all diamond" stance determines that no act shall be considered unmentionable. In the fantasy where the materials which have once covered Edith's navel speak up for themselves, Urine says, "Don't be ashamed." In Book Two the narrator repeatedly urges us to go *beyond his style* (which is to say, in part, beyond the shock of his eroticism) to interpret his truth.

A long lyric passage begins: "God is alive. Magic is afoot," and ends: "This I mean my mind to serve till service is but Magic moving through the world, and mind itself is Magic coursing through the flesh, and flesh itself is Magic dancing on a clock, and time itself the Magic Length of God." (*BL* 158) Questioned by Michael Harris as to his personal stand on religion, Cohen replied that he saw religion as "a technique for strength and for making the universe hospitable." He spoke of the difficulties experienced by many people today in connection with the word "God," and said that for him the word had no negative connotations or organizational associations: "It's easier for me to say God than 'some unnameable mysterious power that motivates all living things.' . . . I can say 'to become close to Him is to feel His grace' because I have felt it."[3] It is interesting to compare this statement with the mood of religious faith which marks the endings of MacLennan's *The Watch That Ends the Night* and *Return of the Sphinx*.

F.'s stance as a professional teacher (his self-description) parallels Breavman's role, in *The Favorite Game*, as artist. Both teacher and artist are truth-seekers, visionaries, iconoclasts and revolutionaries. Political revolution interests F. less than the sexual one, which is dedicated to blowing up traditional Canadian sexual mores. One uproarious scene, where F. is packed in a crowd of demonstrators in Lafontaine Park, connects revolutionary ardour with physical passion: "I knew that all of us, not just the girl and me, all of us were going to come together." (*BL* 121) Just as life and time are an orgasmic "cunt of now," so a nation's pride is described as physical, tangible, something shared rather than private: "It is measured by how many hard-ons live beyond the solitary dream."

F. notes with approval the new sexual consciousness in the Montreal of the sixties, the body-conscious clothing, the physical pride:

They walk differently now, the young men and women of Montreal. Music floats out of manholes. Their clothes are different – no smelly pockets bulging with Kleenex bundles of illegal come. Shoulders are thrown back, organs signal merrily through transparent underwear. . . . There is love on Rue Ste. Catherine, patroness of spinsters. . . .

First secular miracle: La Canadienne, hitherto victim of motel frost, hitherto beloved of nun's democracy, . . . – revolution has done what only wet Hollywood did before. (*BL* 186)

Cohen, like Norman O. Brown and Herbert Marcuse, believes that all parts of the body are erotogenic, or at least have the possibility of so becoming. F.'s credo (and the entire novel suggests that it is also Cohen's) is: "Down with genital imperialism! All flesh can come!" (*BL* 32) Fingers are as erotic as nipples. F. and the narrator's wife Edith invent the Telephone Dance, index fingers in each other's ears. F. says he *became* a telephone, the conductor of Edith's electrical conversation.[4] And what, the narrator asks, did he hear? "Ordinary eternal machinery." The implications of this sexual and metaphysical conceit (played against the narrator's indignant jealousy) are picked up later in connection with the confrontation between Christianity and the Indian religions. A priest instructs his adult Indian pupils, candidates for baptism, to "forget forever the Telephone Dance. . . . As those waxy digits were withdrawn a wall of silence was thrown up between the forest and the hearth, and the old people gathered at the priest's hem shivered with a new kind of loneliness." (*BL* 82) They no longer hear and smell the natural world, growing and dying. The Telephone Dance of human communication through sex is identified with the communication man may have with the cosmos when he is open to its unity and holiness. Cohen charges that the Christian priests, betraying the witness of their own Scripture and forgetting what their mystics have always known, destroyed this natural communication and unity between man and nature. The Iroquois Virgin Catherine works in the opposite direction, restoring the lost unity, "grafting all the fallen branches to the living Tree." (*BL* 210) The living, all-embracing tree is a favourite metaphor in the cabala, and the image here is set in a context of other cabalistic references.

The teacher-pupil-lover relationship between F. and his friend is complicated by the fact that the teacher is also involved in the existential lesson. F. is himself a pupil of life and history: "We lay in each other's arms, each of us the other's teacher." It is further complicated by the fact that both men love Edith, "our Edith," the wife of F.'s friend. Jealousy, as F. informs his friend, is the education his friend has chosen. From time to time the scholarly narrator adjusts his perspective so that he can accept their sharing of Edith: "How quickly pettiness returns, and that most ignoble form of real estate, the possessive occupation and tyranny over two square inches of human flesh, the wife's cunt."(*BL* 13)

In "A Long Letter from F.," F. writes: "I was your journey and you were my journey, and Edith was our holy star." The Morning Star images the eternal polarity between the sexes in D.H. Lawrence's *The Plumed Serpent.* Perhaps the passage is intended as a Lawrencian parody, for Cohen's genuinely lyric passages are handled differently. F. eulogizes the androgynous man. Homosexuality, latent in Lawrence's fiction and unabashed in Cohen's, is credited with strengthening both individual integrity and heterosexual love: "Our queer love keeps the lines of our manhood hard and clean, so that we bring nobody but our own self to our separate marriage beds, and our women finally know us." (*BL* 154)

The weekend which F. and Edith spend in the Argentine is one long and glorious spoof on sex, complete with a sex-stimulator machine called a Danish Vibrator, and a mad waiter who has nothing on beneath his spy-type raincoat. By writing all the gory details to his friend, F. intends to prepare him for the "pilgrimage" of life, and urges his friend to go beyond his own petty experiences: "Here is a plea based on my whole experience: do not be a magician, be magic." (*BL* 164) Do not be a philosopher-teacher: just live.

The narrative fantasy, where F. is physician and instructor to a frigid Edith, piles parody upon parody. It parodies the Pygmalion myth and, simultaneously, the novel's own theme of ironic failure: "all my Pygmalion tampering, it means nothing, I know now . . . you were beyond my gadgetry." (*BL* 183) F. is the physician who cannot heal himself, the Moses who will never see the Promised Land. It parodies the role of teacher, through a box-within-box technique: Charles Axis (mythic strong man of an advertising culture, immaculate in a white bathing suit) is to F. what F. is to his friend and to Edith. It parodies the melodramatic formula of the eternal triangle in Edith's angry tirade: "I hate you for what you've done to me and my husband. I was a fool to get mixed up with you." It parodies the style and phrasing of sex manuals, or the advertising material which accompanies the Danish Vibrator: "CASE HISTORIES AND intensive field work. Filled with chapters detailing ALL ASPECTS of the sex act. SAMPLE HEADINGS: Rubbing, Seeing, Silk Rings. . . . " (*BL* 169)

Nothing is sacred. The historical record of the tortures of the Jesuits Brébeuf and Lalemant is recited by F. to assist Edith towards orgasm. The conventional moralist will now shut the book with a snap, if indeed he has made it thus far. But cruelty *can* excite human beings sexually.[5] *The Favorite Game* explores at some length the sadistic streak which is evident in children, and is an element in the human psyche. This is *us,* Cohen is saying, or at least *part* of us. Let's not pretend we are something better than we are. The whole hilarious Argentinian incident is Cohen the immoral moralist at his best.

Cohen looks at his society and dislikes what he sees. He sees pain and mutilation everywhere, "throats ripped with greed," thousands squashed on highways in a "wrecked world," compulsive tooth-brushers (intimidated by an advertising culture which subverts hygiene to its own profit), scholars unhappily impaled upon the thorns of research (hyperbole again?) – in short, a wilderness, a demonic society. Hence F.'s urgency: "Caution was a luxury. There was no time for me to examine my motives. Self-purification would have been an alibi. Beholding such a spectacle of misery, I was free to try anything. I can't answer for my own erection. . . . Change! Purify! Experiment! Cauterize! Reverse! Burn! Preserve! Teach!" (*BL* 174–5)

The long paragraph continues in this vein, as F. pictures himself as Dr. Frankenstein with a deadline. The running motif of Charles Axis and the ideal body is a comic and satiric metaphor for human perfection. F. recognizes that he himself is part of the disaster, this mutilated, fearful society from which he is painfully attempting to extract himself. Truth and fun. The whole mock critique of society is in the crazy context of F.'s and Edith's jealous struggle for the Danish Vibrator. The prophet mocks himself and his own role, accepting his weaknesses and failures – with laughter.

The weekend "therapy" climaxes in the escape of the Danish Vibrator. Battery-less, it seems to have a life of its own. The Vibrator's escape parodies old Frankenstein movies, science fiction, prayer, and sentimental melodrama. The machine makes its incredible way across the room, stopping only for one last assault upon Edith. It heads for the window, "straps and cups flowing behind it, like a Hawaiian skirt made of grass and brassieres." (*BL* 178) It crashes through the glass, purring and moaning, and crosses the parking lot to the beach. A man wearing an immaculate white bathing suit (Charles Axis, of course) watches its graceful progress towards the water and its descent below the waves. Will it return, asks Edith breathlessly? F. pronounces the benediction: "It doesn't matter. It's in the world."

Has Cohen any purpose in the Vibrator incident, beyond sheer fun and defence of pleasure? I think he has. F. admits that Edith is *beyond* his gadgetry. Gadgets can come to possess a life of their own, and to dominate their makers. The "sound" given off by men, in the fantasy with which F.'s long letter begins, is "Shhh." This sound, described as male, is the very opposite of the sound made by women, and F.'s preference for women has been identified with his love of the world. It is clear from the associations made by F. that this male sound represents the technological culture by which man attempts to order and control the world:

Shhh, and the roofs are raised against the storm. Shhh, the forests are cleared so the wind will not rattle the trees. Shhh, the hydrogen rockets go off to silence dissent and variety. . . . Shhh, it whispers to the white chaos, lie down in dormitory rows. Shhh, it implores the dancing molecules, I love dances but I do not love foreign dances, I love dances that have rules, my rules. (*BL* 147)

How subtly technology progresses, from private houses to hydrogen rockets and the silencing of all dissent: follow my rules, friend – or I will destroy you. Of course women can be technocrats and exploiters as well as men. But in our mid-twentieth-century, North American culture, women still form a very small minority among those in power in the technological society. So Cohen uses the traditional archetype of man controlling and woman submitting, for his denunciation of our manipulative society.

One of the most striking, and gruesome, scenes in *Beautiful Losers* is the nineteenth episode in Book One, the impotent rape of Edith at the age of thirteen. Anyone who doubts that Cohen is a moralist should read this scene. The girl-child here is the archetypal Victim: child, woman, Indian in a white society, naïve consumer in an exploiting culture dependent upon extravagant consumption. The narrator identifies the child-victim about to be mutilated with Canadian resources and culture. Rape is the ultimate metaphor for exploitation. The Quebec forests are mutilated and sold to America; the saplings are murdered: "Bittersweet is the cunt sap of a thirteen-year-old." Oh yes, the narrator admits, he knows about war and business, he is aware of shit, and aware that he is part of it. He still wants us to see it for what it really *is*.

Genocide is the bitter underside to the beautiful losers theme. Cohen's F. believes that White America has "destroyed the Red Man and stolen his pleasures." (*BL* 89) The Telephone Dance – remember? He believes, further, that the Americans are now doing to the English-Canadians what the English did to the French, and what both French and English did to the Indian. So the chain of destruction and exploitation goes on. The chain of cultural rape.

"French Canadian school books do not encourage respect for the Indians," the narrator says in the rape scene. Cohen, by the way, neither whitewashes nor idealizes the Indians: they were cruel; they sometimes ate one another: it's all there in the novel. But religious intolerance has an ugly face. Edith has been abused by schoolmates who did not think she was Christian. Her attackers are surprised to discover clean underwear: "a heathen's underwear should be limp and smeared."

Edith runs through the wood, thirteen years old, with four men after her. The village was "behind" the men, an ambiguous phrase applicable on literal and psychological levels. The village supports the action of the men. This meaning is developed as the scene proceeds. The Collective Will commands, indeed delegates, the men to "Get Edith!" Why Edith?

Can't you see what is behind all this teen-age advertising? Is it only money? What does "wooing the teen-age market" really mean? . . . Dying America wants a thirteen-year-old Abishag to warm its bed. . . . O suffering child-lust offices of the business world, I feel your blue-balled pain everywhere! . . . Advertising courts lovely things. (*BL* 58–9)

The psychological manipulation of children and adolescents by advertising encourages precocious sexual maturity. Cohen is a master of mood, and of the tension produced by the juxtaposition of moods. In the quoted passage, hatred of others jostles with hatred of self, with humorous acceptance, and wry acknowledgment of facts.

The terrified Edith urinates. The sound of urine falling on dry leaves and pine needles is "a holy symbol of frailty," inviolate. The men's erections collapse. But they refuse to cooperate with what F. calls a miracle, and attack the child with fingers, pipes, pens, twigs. An impotent attack by dying America, an aged King David. The attack takes place in an abandoned quarry, "owned indirectly by U.S. interests." Cohen pictures an impotent America capable of destruction but not of creation. Infertile. He returns to the attack on the U.S. in "A Long Letter from F.," after his tribute to the sexually liberated Canadienne: "I want to hammer a beautiful coloured bruise on the whole American monolith. . . . I want the edge of a tin can to drink America's throat. I want two hundred million to know that everything can be different, any old different." (*BL* 186–7) Hyperbole? Certainly. Moderation has never been Cohen's style.

Germaine Greer's denunciation of the consumer emphasis which underlies the stereotyped image of the female parallels Cohen's use, in the rape episode, of the female as archetypal victim. The female stereotype, Greer argues, is a sexless object, a non-person, a con-sumer only in order that, as a beautiful product, she herself may be consumed by men: "The men of our civilization have stripped them-selves of the fineries of earth so that they might work more freely to plunder the universe for treasures to deck my lady in. . . . My lady must therefore be the chief spender as well as the chief symbol of spending ability and monetary success."[6] Miss Greer's remark is already dated, in part, as the men of the seventies seem to have decided to join the women in exotic finery and conspicuous waste.

A raped girl, and an exploited land. Cohen is very much a man of his times in his pro-Canadian stance. MacLennan's nationalism in the forties was prophetic, a voice crying in the wilderness long be-fore it was a common concern. By the mid-sixties (yes, my friend, it took that long, to paraphrase F.'s remark about his sexual education) Canadians were just beginning to realize that their very existence as a nation was endangered by American economic and cultural imper-ialism. They were also waking up to the plight of their native peoples and to a consciousness of guilt for the way in which the Eskimo and the Indian have been and still are being treated. Note that the means of rape, in the episode with the adolescent Edith, are non-human. Technology, as Jacques Ellul reminds us, expands by its own inner momentum; ultimately, its sphere extends to include everything: "not only are material objects subordinated to technics, but man also. The latter is no longer subject, he becomes in his turn the object of the forces which he has created."[7]

The narrator, in his search for the long-dead Iroquois Virgin Catherine, finds that he has "stumbled on the truth about Canada." Canada, the raped Indian girl, is also the mutilated Indian saint. The narrator wonders whether all his loves must be mutilated. And what does mutilation mean, beyond the religious and economic aspects already explored? Catherine's name means "she who puts things in order," "she who, advancing, arranges the shadows neatly." The nar-rator wonders why, with her instinctive love of the natural world, her vision never turned Rabelaisian. Catherine is *puritan* in be-haviour. She loves work, she disdains play, disdains sex, disdains to adorn herself with the embroidery and handicraft she sews for others. This behaviour the Church enthusiastically endorses: "O Sinister Church!" In a serio-comic peroration, the narrator sees both him-self and F. as victims of "the system," and drives home the charges implicit earlier: "I accuse the Roman Catholic Church of Quebec of ruining my sex life. . . . I accuse the Church of female circumcision in French Canada." (*BL* 47)[8] Puritanism, that is to say, made an atmosphere where physical pleasure became an impossibility.

In the winter of 1680, when Catherine lay dying, the priests were uncertain as to whether they should break one of their established customs. They were in the habit of taking the sick to the Sacrament in the chapel, not the Sacrament to the sick where they lay: "they longed for a Jesus of Canada dignified by convention and antiquity, as He is today, pale and plastic above the guilty traffic tickets." (*BL* 207) A plastic Jesus. An artificial, synthetic and utterly dead Jesus. Cohen's picture of the Church in the sixties may be less hyperbolic than churchmen would like to think. Canadians who value the life of their religious heritage should take another look at the dead hand of dignified conventions, while remembering another one of F.'s dictums: "A strong man cannot but love the Church." (*BL* 5)

Who are the beautiful losers? The four main characters of the novel, certainly. And the rest of us too, for Cohen's losers become a metaphor for the human condition, the "poor men, poor men, such as we" of the novel's closing paragraph. *To live is to fail*, as the novel reminds us, without tears. Life is a beautiful failure, an ironic success. F. suggests that to feel oneself a Negro is the best feeling that anyone can have today. His novel celebrates the archetypal dream: "for we do not wish to destroy the past and its baggy failures, we only wish the miracles to demonstrate that the past was joyously prophetic, and that possibility occurs to us most plainly on this cargo deck of wide lapels." (*BL* 215)

Edith belongs to the Indian tribe of A——s, whose brief history is one of incessant defeat; she ends as a suicide. F. refers to his own failure repeatedly. At the end of his long letter he points to failure as a goal, claiming to have lost almost everything, and achieved humility. He is doomed to offend, to be misunderstood, and to participate in the very things he chooses to condemn. The narrator is a disillusioned scholar, an authority on the A——s (which is to say, on failure), who says his interest in "this pack of failures" betrays his character. He has failed to love properly his wife and friend. His constipation, which seals him off from the universe within his own appetite, is a comic image of failure at the most basic level of life. He lists his failures hyperbolically, sitting in misery upon "the porcelain machine."

Cohen is a poet, in his novels as in his poetry. His Rabelaisian moods are complemented by delicate lyric passages, although the lyricism may be consciously undercut at any point: "A robin listened

as she wept, a fucking robin stopped in his tracks and listened."
Cohen uses the virgin Catherine, mutilated in childhood by the
plague, as a lyric version of the failure–success theme. After death,
her face is physically transfigured from battered swarthiness to clear
white beauty. The transfiguration is Cohen's metaphor for the
losers' sea-change into something rare and strange, beyond the
failure of death.

As a Jew in French Montreal in Canada, Cohen knows what it is
to be isolated. The year 1965, when he embarked on *Beautiful
Losers*, was a bad one for Cohen. In 1970 he told interviewer Susan
Lumsden that he felt he *had* to write that book. He was at the end
of his resources, hating himself, needing to prove himself as a
writer. He sat down to his desk and decided to use only the books
that were there: a rare book on Catherine Tekakwitha that a friend
had given him, a 1943 Blue Beetle comic book, and a few others.
"I think it's the best thing I've ever done. It's a technical master-
piece."[9]

The closing pages of F.'s long letter are a fantastic and gro-
tesquely humorous celebration of failure. Cohen's technique provides a parody of the electronic media of the sixties, which is at the
same time his subject. F. sits in the System Theatre in the last feature. The projection beam becomes a ghostly white snake, "the first
snake in the shadows of the original garden . . . offering our female
memory the taste of – everything!" F. dares himself to imagine the
newsreel escaping into the feature, thereby eliminating the seem-
ingly impenetrable wall between fiction and non-fiction, art and
life. Cohen proceeds to illustrate F.'s fantasy, through the radio
bulletin of a police pursuit of F. (who has suddenly become an
unidentified terrorist leader) and the O.T. nurse. The pursuit, complete with police dogs and messages concealed within the body,
parodies a spy thriller. The radio comes to life (like the Danish
Vibrator, earlier) and demands revenge. Melodrama, science fiction, pornography, McLuhan's media, and contemporary North
American culture are reduced to an ultimate absurdity: "Run, F.
Run for all of us A—s!" The teacher-prophet escapes, that he may
continue to tell it like it is for all of us beautiful losers.

NOTES

1. Don Owen, "Leonard Cohen: The Poet as Hero. 3," *Saturday Night* (June 1969), p. 32.

2. See Robert Fulford, "A wave of absurdist fiction is making the Canadian scene," *Ottawa Citizen* (October 9, 1971), p. 36: "A wave of absurdist fiction is making a rather late appearance on the Canadian scene – there were earlier examples in Leonard Cohen's *Beautiful Losers* and Mordecai Richler's *Cocksure*. . . . Now the absurdists – Martin Myers, Leo Simpson and Matt Cohen are three others – are arriving in some force. We can expect more, because clearly the anarchic vision appeals to our writers as a way of dealing with a world in which, as they see it, traditional values have come to have no meaning."

3. Michael Harris, "Leonard Cohen: The Poet as Hero. 2," *Saturday Night* (June 1969), p. 30.

4. Cohen's metaphor is by no means far-fetched. Recent studies by Russian physiologists indicate the electric potential of the skin and have verified the basic claims for acupuncture in traditional Chinese medicine. See Stephan Palos, *The Chinese Art of Healing* (New York: Herder and Herder, 1971), Foreword by William Gutman, M.D., p. viii: "The skin might be thought of as a screen on which the inner organs are projected through nerve connections; or as part of a *telephone relay system* in which the stimulation of a certain point by a pin prick spreads through reflex action to the nerve-connected inner organ [italics mine]."

5. Cf. Hugh MacLennan, *The Watch That Ends the Night*, p. 174: " 'Those fights were a substitute for sex,' Jerome said. 'That greedy look of a crowd of sex-hungry men watching a fight. It's in us, George, it's in us. Once I saw a man flogged. . . . Why the man was flogged I never knew, but he was, and the men were for it.' "

6. Germaine Greer, *The Female Eunuch* (London: Paladin, 1971), pp. 55-6.

7. Jacques Ellul, *The Presence of the Kingdom* (New York: Seabury, 1967), p. 76.

8. In the Muslim areas of the Middle East, female circumcision is sometimes performed upon girls before they reach puberty. The female is thus made incapable of experiencing pleasure in the sexual act.

9. Susan Lumsden, "Leonard Cohen Wants the 'Unconditional Leadership of the World,' " *Weekend Magazine* (September 12, 1970), p. 24.

9 'LIFE IS A GIFT'

"The novelist's principal aim is to celebrate life": in Heather Methuen and Paul Tallard's discussion of the novelist's purpose, MacLennan reveals his own ideal. He too intends to celebrate life. *The Watch That Ends the Night* is a great affirmative statement, where characters who are puritan by MacLennan's definition (George's Aunt Agnes, who blights his early life, and the disapproving parishioners of Giles Martell) play a very minor role. And yet MacLennan has remained within the tradition of historic Puritanism, as suggested in Chapter Three. His moral seriousness is woven into the fabric of this novel, where his primary intention is to make a philosophic and spiritual affirmation about the meaning of life. He intends to guide the reader to see life in similar terms, and the tone of the novel becomes evangelistic in the closing chapters. MacLennan hopes to encourage in his reader a spirit of reverence towards life, a spirit of acceptance and gratitude for such a gift. We are not far from the teachings of Albert Schweitzer, nor, indeed, from the teachings of the New Testament, which is frequently quoted by MacLennan.

This moral seriousness is apparent in all of MacLennan's novels. In *The Watch That Ends the Night*, however, there is a new sense of the complexity and mysteriousness of morality, truth and duty. "What is my duty?" Jerome asks George Stewart. There are no simple explanations for anything, as George has learned on his trip to Russia. MacLennan aims, here, not at a literature of understanding but rather at a literature of truth which cannot be pinned down, as George describes the great Russian literature. Thus MacLennan's affirmation in *The Watch* is not intended as a definition or even as an explanation, but rather as a gospel or proclamation of good news: that life is a gift to be accepted with reverent gratitude.

George Stewart is the novel's narrator and the confidant of all the other characters. His is the central intelligence, the prevailing point of view, like Henry James' Strether in *The Ambassadors*, or Conrad's Marlowe in *Heart of Darkness* and *Lord Jim*. He contrasts excellently, as Peter Buitenhuis notes, with Jerome Martell, whose fantastic abilities are filtered through George's quiet observations.[1]

George is a seeker, as Daniel Ainslie is in *Each Man's Son*. They are pupils who must learn life's lesson. As Ainslie was taught by old Dr. MacKenzie, and by suffering, so George is taught by his "spiritual father" Jerome Martell, by Catherine, and by Catherine's illness, which is "fate palpable." Like Daniel, George hardens his heart against his early teaching; he refuses to learn, or is incapable of so doing until taught by suffering. Jerome Martell's childhood experiences, as told to George, provide a basic metaphor throughout the novel. George remembers Jerome's experiences during various crises of his own, and they acquire for George a progressively deeper meaning, illuminating the actions of both Jerome and himself.

Jerome has spent his childhood in an isolated lumber camp in New Brunswick. His mother was the camp's cook, and almost the only woman in the area. She ruled the camp as queen and despot. Jerome never knew his father or his surname. One March night when Jerome was ten his mother was murdered by one of her lovers, whom Jerome calls the Engineer. MacLennan shows us that the brutality of Jerome's mother, her total lack of sympathy, is responsible for driving the Engineer almost to temporary insanity. The murder and the events which lead to it symbolize for Jerome all the violence and evil of the world. Earlier, Jerome has told George that he considers cruelty to be the ultimate evil. In *Each Man's Son* there is another murderous fight to which a horrified boy is witness, and which becomes for him the archetype of all violence. In *The Watch*, the responsibility which Jerome's mother bears for bringing violence upon herself represents the responsibility which humanity should recognize that it bears for the evils it brings upon itself. When we refuse to love, we destroy ourselves.

After the murder of his mother, Jerome escapes down the river in his small bark canoe. Swollen with melting snow, the river is rushing to the ocean. Jerome draws ashore just before the open gulf, and hides on a train which takes him down the eastern side of New Brunswick. Filthy and starving, he is found in the railway station at Moncton and adopted by the Martells, a childless couple who are among MacLennan's most delightful creations. Giles Martell, a Protestant clergyman, is addicted to drink. He describes his profession as an unpopular one, its chief disadvantage lying in the fact that his parishioners have such a poor view of their Master's intelligence that they deny in their minds that he was in earnest when he turned the water into wine at Cana.

Jerome's story (Part Five) contains some of MacLennan's best writing – tense, dramatic, humanly real, spiritually significant. The Martells, especially Josephine, embody the author's affirmation. As Jerome tells George, his foster father was probably the only genuine Christian he will ever meet in his life. Jerome stresses the acceptance of his foster mother – a loving, thankful and uncritical acceptance. She accepts the filthy nameless boy as a God-given gift. Similarly, she accepts her husband's drinking, understanding that it is a necessity to help him overcome his guilt and religious fear: "She took it, George, she took it," Jerome adds, with the Hemingway touch. It is this attitude of grateful acceptance for whatever life may bring which is the lesson George is to learn, and MacLennan illustrates it clearly in the person of Josephine Martell.

We are told that Martell means "hammer." Doctor and soldier, mystic healer and warrior, Jerome is one of MacLennan's most interesting characters, certainly his most forceful one. Jerome bears a striking resemblance to Norman Bethune, Canadian surgeon and medical advisor in 1938 to the people's United Front Government of China. But Buitenhuis notes that "MacLennan asserts that he did not know of Bethune when writing the book, did not even hear of him, in fact, until it was nearly finished."[2] After his death in 1939 at the age of forty-nine, Bethune became a legendary figure[3] known throughout the world as soldier, surgeon, painter, poet and "something of a missionary," in his own laconic understatement. In the Introduction to the 1971 revised edition of *The Scalpel, the Sword*, a biography of Bethune written by Ted Allan and Sydney Gordon, the authors take objection to their hero being turned by a contemporary Canadian novelist (whom they do not name) into an "anti-Bethune figure" and a "disillusioned idealist who winds up broken and defeated." Allan and Gordon presumably have in mind MacLennan's Jerome Martell. Their interpretation of Jerome's stance at the end of *The Watch* appears to me as totally inaccurate, for Jerome has triumphed over his defeat. The novelist's artistic truth, moreover, is quite different from the biographer's frame of reference, so that even if MacLennan's Jerome were shown as defeated it would be no reflection on Bethune.

The two sides of Jerome's nature, kindness and pugnacity, are represented by his two professions. Through *Foxe's Book of Martyrs*, read as a child, Jerome has learned that torture calls for martyrs, by which he means that bullies must be resisted, else torture becomes the way of the world. In the first half of his life, Jerome's resistance is active. He goes to Spain to support the Loyalist forces resisting Franco's Fascists. This has not been an easy decision for Jerome to make. He tells George more than once that it is not easy to be him. After his return, however, Jerome's resistance becomes an active passivity. Christ-like, he suffers rather than fights, and by suffering the results of evil in his own person he turns evil to good.

In the thirties, Jerome, like many idealists at the time, became convinced that he should go to help the Loyalists in the Spanish Civil War. Jerome is caught here in a terrible dilemma. On the one hand, he feels that in a time of mass suffering he has no right to personal happiness, no right to put the desires of himself and his family before the needs of the thousands who need medical help in Spain. The happiness of his wife and daughter, moreover, depend upon his helping to make the world "safe" by resisting Fascist bullies in Spain. On the other hand, however, there is a chance that his wife's delicate heart may not survive the shock of his leaving. Hence his question to George: what is my duty? His quick kindness cannot resist Shatwell's plea to help the widow Martha, who has been operated on unsuccessfully by Dr. Rodgers, the head of Jerome's hospital. His quick pugnacity cannot resist the opportunity for battle at a communist rally. Thus the two sides of Jerome's impulsive nature lead him, irresistibly, to the point where Dr. Rodgers demands his resignation from the hospital. His very vitality has forced a solution to his dilemma over Spain.

Excluded from the hospital, he feels that his choice has been made for him. Is he betraying Catherine? He honestly feels that he does not know. He tells George that a man must belong to something larger than himself. God was convenient for that purpose when people could believe in him: "Now there is nothing but people." This is Jerome's explanation for his motives at the time when he leaves for Spain. Catherine and Mrs. Martell have another explanation. Jerome has described to George the horror of his war experiences when he was only eighteen. His memory of the last victim of his bayonet, a blond German boy, is particularly vivid. Catherine tells George of Jerome's guilt feelings in this connection, and her conviction that his war experiences resurfaced when war erupted in Spain. The Depression had already killed Jerome's earlier gaiety, as he identified with the sufferings of the unemployed.

He tells George that disease begins in economic conditions, in the malnutrition and insecurity of the slums, the "whole damned nineteenth century set-up Sir Rupert Irons represents." In *Barometer Rising*, Neil MacRae mounts a similar attack on the slums of Halifax; and Heather Methuen, in *Two Solitudes*, tends to feel guilty because of the existence of the poor. This is all part of MacLennan's idealism and of his hope for a better world.

Jerome's guilt feelings in the Depression have been reinforced by the Spanish War. Mrs. Martell writes to Catherine that he has left her because of the war, combined with the traumatic effects of his mother's murder. But Mrs. Martell continues with a deeper explanation as she begs Catherine to "pray that he may discover the peace he seeks, and that he will find God before it is too late because that is what he *really* seeks, for if he finds God he will find himself, and then he will find *you*." (*WE* 312) This is close to Jerome's own final interpretation of his going to Spain: he was trying to run away from himself. And this, he tells George, is what George is trying to do during Catherine's illness.

George is a quiet contemplative man who comes to see in Jerome's childhood experience the symbol for his own fate and that of his generation. The orphan archetype, with its concurrent images of wandering and seeking, is found throughout MacLennan's fiction. Jerome's frail bark canoe, driven relentlessly forward on the spring flood towards ocean depths, becomes the dominating metaphor of the novel: "A canoe in an ocean at night, with a hurricane rising. Jerome, Myself, Everyone." (*WE* 289) George's self-confidence has been ruined in youth by the disparaging criticism of his Aunt Agnes. Her work has been reinforced by his experiences in the Depression and by his unfulfilled love for Catherine. He loses sight of her for many years, and when their friendship is renewed in Montreal he finds that Catherine has married Jerome Martell. George also finds that he has never ceased to love her. When Jerome goes to Spain, the shock leaves Catherine shaken and ill. George shares her suffering and is overwhelmed by his own mixed reaction to the whole situation: "Now I, too, was at sea, and I thought of that vast reservoir of emotions and memories on which every fragile human life floats." (*WE* 315)

Several years go by and George's confidence is now, as he thinks, well-established. In 1941, news comes that Jerome has been tortured to death by the Nazis. George asks Catherine to marry him, and she refuses. She says that she is not equal to love, which is an exhausting force; George must find someone else. Catherine now feels that, in one way, she and Jerome failed one another by loving too much. Their love was mutually exhausting, with each demanding from the other more than was possible. She asks George if he knows the line from Rilke, "Love consists in this, that two solitudes protect and touch and greet each other," and adds that a marriage based on that kind of love could last.[4] George realizes that Catherine is trying to tell him that love must not be overly dependent or possessive, and that love sought as an escape from the burden of self becomes a captivity.

But George is still unable to accept this lesson, although he finally comes to do so. He hardens his heart, as Daniel Ainslie does when Dr. MacKenzie tells him he is seeking a god, not a son, and when Daniel himself first realizes that Mollie cannot be pushed aside and ignored. As Daniel continues in his effort to dominate Alan, so George continues in his effort to escape from himself. He is convinced that he *wants* the captivity of love. When Catherine has been given confirmation of Jerome's death, and when she becomes convinced that George will never marry anyone else, she agrees to marry George. In the last two chapters of Part Six, MacLennan shows, first, the heights of happiness, then the depths of despair: like the turn of the dragonfly's wing, so rapid the change. MacLennan uses this line from classical Greek poetry in both *The Watch* and *Two Solitudes*, as an image of the rapid reversal of fortune which may strike when a man least expects it. Chapter Eleven is a brief but striking epithalamium, George and Catherine's marriage song of sheer joy: "She, who had said 'yes' with all her might to Jerome, now said 'yes' to me." (*WE* 321) George and Catherine know that their time is short, but they live in joyful acceptance of the present. Catherine's joy in her painting, her riot of colour, reflects her joy in living.

In Chapter Twelve, the key changes from joy to pity and terror. Catherine suffers her first embolism. She recovers, thanks to the enormous life force in her which mystifies even the doctors. But as a result of her embolism, George and Catherine live with a feeling of the sword hanging over their heads, a feeling of "beyond-this-nothing." George and Catherine, like the characters in Albert Camus' *The Plague*, actually share their plight with Everyman. Like Everyman, George seeks to avoid facing this knowledge until circumstances force the recognition. Catherine recovers, and George thinks he is equal to living with her illness. By the ending of Part Six, MacLennan has brought us, with numerous flashbacks, to the point at which the novel began, the winter when Jerome returns from the dead.

In retrospect George realizes that he has not known what his true position was at that time, but he is soon to discover it. In Part Seven, Jerome is presented by MacLennan as a Christ-figure, a man who has returned from the dead and has acquired, through suffering and self-surrender, mysterious powers to heal both body and soul. Jerome has been missing for ten years, and was pronounced dead. He has spent those ten years in concentration camps, tortured and ill. His fighting instinct has continued to assert itself against torture and apparent hopelessness: "Always he had been driven on just as he had been driven down the river in his canoe that night in his boyhood. . . . But his constitution resisted death, and his mind after virtually dying became active again." (*WE* 329) The new Jerome has a strange and healing effect upon everyone with whom he comes in contact. Jerome suffers the hate of Harry Blackwell to be poured out upon himself, leaving Harry cleansed, healed and restored. Jerome absorbs George's fear, the fear of death which is really a fear of life. George feels that Jerome is inside him, that he *is* him, with the result that a murderous feeling departs from George and he is finally left peaceful, happy and sure of his own identity. New Testament stories of the casting out of devils come irresistibly to mind in connection with this incident. Jerome sits beside Catherine after her operation, and feels death brush past him out of the room.

George's basic terror is due to loss of faith. As a child, he had been taught to regard God as a loving Father. George feels that Catherine's illness proves that God is indifferent, for Catherine's character is not responsible for her fate. When a man loses his image of God as a loving Father, he looks for substitutes, such as family, work, political systems. But none of these substitutes abides: "Then, though we may deny it, comes the Great Fear. For if a man cannot believe that he serves more than himself, if he cannot believe there is meaning in the human struggle, what are his chances of emotional survival?" (*WE* 342) His chances, MacLennan indicates, are very slim indeed. Human dignity demands the belief that there *is* meaning to the human struggle. George is to discover what he believes every man must know and feel, "if he is to live with a sense of how utterly tremendous is the mystery our ancestors confidently called God." (*WE* 324)

This is the first novel where MacLennan has so clearly stated man's need for God, although he remains chary of the word itself. In *Each Man's Son*, Ainslie is told that he seeks a god, not a son; despite this, Ainslie is given a son and not a god. True, Ainslie must first learn that love must be accepting and giving, not possessive and demanding, as George learns in *The Watch*. But the ultimate value which MacLennan presents in *Each Man's Son* is not God, but a loving human being, in comparison with which "everything else is worthless." Similarly, in *The Precipice*, MacLennan suggests that Stephen must lose his guilt feelings. But how? MacLennan does not imply that Stephen is in need of a god. Stephen's solution, presumably, is somehow to take a firm hand with himself and convince himself of his own innocence.

In *The Watch*, however, MacLennan states that man's emotional survival demands faith in some form. Jerome frequently asserts that man must belong to something larger than himself. In the cathedral hush and beauty of a Canadian autumn, George comes to understand that to learn to love the mystery around him is the final sanction of human existence:

All our lives we had wanted to belong to something larger than ourselves. We belonged consciously to nothing now except to the pattern of our lives and fates. To God, possibly. I am chary of using that much mis-used word, but I say honestly that at least I was conscious of his power. Whatever the spirit might be I did not know, but I knew it was there. Life was a gift. . . . Remembering the years when she had wrung life and joy out of pain and perpetual exhaustion, I knew, deep inside, that this struggle was not valueless. (*WE* 372-3)

After this affirmation, MacLennan closes with the New Testament parable of the talents, and the Lord's promise to the faithful servant to enter into the joy of the Lord.

George has learned what great musicians have always known: that life is a continuing cycle of destruction and re-creation into new harmonies; that the final one is "a will to live, love, grow and be grateful, the determination to endure all things, suffer all things, hope all things, believe all things necessary for what our ancestors called the glory of God." (*WE* 344) It makes no difference that God appears to be indifferent to man's idea of justice, and no difference whether the gift of life is for many years or for an hour. The sun's warmth, the air's softness, the flower's beauty, the miracle of growth: the finite passing quality of these things is one with their permanent value. One thinks of D.H. Lawrence in this connection. As he neared the end of his life, Lawrence wrote: "Whatever the unborn and the dead may know, they cannot know the beauty, the marvel of being alive in the flesh." With his health rapidly failing, Lawrence joyously affirmed the value of the flesh and physical things, while his own personal battle witnessed to the spirit.

We have seen in MacLennan's earlier novels the affirmation that sex is right and good, normal and healthy, but only under certain conditions. "Little children, love one another," Matt McCunn tells Lucy in *The Precipice*, as he mocks the innocence of those who think that sex is the only sin. His attitude is a major factor in helping her realize she must take a chance and marry Stephen, must reject her puritan background in order to accept life. But some years later Lucy realizes that while sex is natural and good between Stephen and herself, it is "obscene and terrible and unjust" when it concerns Stephen and Gail. Similarly, Bruce Fraser realizes that he must cauterize his mind of Lucy's beauty and presence; he cannot encourage his love for her since she is married to Stephen Lassiter. The same moral attitudes may be discerned in *The Watch That Ends the Night*, but with an important difference. By the late fifties, MacLennan has a new confidence and ease in his writing about sex. He is through battling for emancipation from what he considers to be puritan inhibitions in Canadian society. The old moralism is reflected in Catherine and Jerome's restraint when Jerome returns from the dead. Catherine has remarried and it is "too late" for them to share physical love. As for the apparently uninhibited intellectuals who use sex as a symbol of rebellion, or to prove an economic theory, Adam Blore on two occasions describes this attitude as puritan. Similarly, Dennis Morey in *Two Solitudes* describes as puritan the men who consider sex the subject for a dirty joke. A contempt for the body and its desires is basic to contemporary puritanism, so that those who indulge bodily desires to excess actually share the same basic attitude as those who condemn any indulgence at all. MacLennan associates this contempt for the body with the type of puritanism which he is attacking.

The desire to mortify the flesh, however, is much older than the seventeenth century. It belongs to the whole ascetic tradition of Christianity. The aim of Christian denial is to express love and obedience: ascetic denial may be a means for one individual to draw closer to God, and for every Christian the denial of his own needs may enable him to assuage the needs of others. Asceticism has a value, then, when it is an act of love under obedience to God. There is a dualistic belief (heretical to Christianity and called, variously, Manichaean, Catharist, Gnostic) which subverts this aim of ascetic denial by suggesting that denial is good in itself, because the world and the flesh are evil in themselves. Such dualism associates God only with spirit, symbolized by light, and abandons matter (the body and the natural world) as evil. The soul's salvation is to escape from the matter which imprisons it. The Christian heresies reflect a universal tendency to sublimate man and to dispose of his finite life in the flesh as unimportant. It is an attitude towards which an idealistic mind is often irresistibly attracted.

In Part Seven of *The Watch*, MacLennan is ambivalent with respect to the ultimate value of the body and the natural order. While he does celebrate the physical world and its beauty, the miracle of life and growth, it seems clear throughout Part Seven of *The Watch* that for MacLennan the final reality is spirit, spirit which excludes and is independent of the body. MacLennan has described this novel as being dependent not on character-in-action but on spirit-in-action, the essential conflict being "between the human spirit of Everyman and Everyman's human condition."[5] I am not suggesting that the author consciously thinks of matter as evil; but there are many hints in the closing chapters that matter is unimportant and even unreal. The faces of Catherine and Jerome are both frequently described as "transparent." The power of Catherine's spirit makes George feel physically "annihilated." The withering of Catherine's body to gossamer frailty is, of course, related to her terrible illness, but it seems in the final analysis to stem more from this dualistic tendency than from the actual illness: "She was so transparent . . . she was alive and yet she was not; she was half-translated and yet she was still here." (*WE* 372) In the final chapters there are innumerable references to light. And at the end, as George anticipates "the joy of the Lord" for both Catherine and himself, he feels that his work and the world itself are "unreal." The joy of the Lord is "light," and the world surrounding George "was becoming a shadow." Such continual references to light, transparency and unreality suggest an underlying dualistic tendency.

MacLennan's references to Jerome's vision of Jesus belong to this pattern. Jerome, in his prison cell, has "virtually" died and come alive again; in an effort to retain his sanity, he has set himself to recall the Gospels, memorized during his boyhood. He tells George that one day he woke and felt Jesus himself in the cell with him: "He wasn't the Jesus who had died for our sins. He was simply a man who had died and risen again. Who had died outwardly as I had died inwardly." (*WE* 330) Later, when George is feeling the effects of Jerome's mysterious healing powers, Jerome refers to Jesus' death and rebirth once more, but with a significant addition: "His spirit rose." MacLennan cannot believe in the resurrection of the body, only of the spirit. And if there is no resurrection of the body, then spirit appears as the final value. The traditional Christian fusion of body and spirit depends upon the doctrine of the

Incarnation. When spirit has penetrated matter and fused to make a new creation, then matter can be the true expression of spirit. *The Watch That Ends the Night* is one of MacLennan's finest novels. Peter Buitenhuis acknowledges its power, while criticizing the moralizing turn taken at the end: "In the last section of the book, the narrator's voice becomes less authentic. . . . The author's voice comes through too insistently, and the illusion of the novel collapses among a heap of morals."[6] I suspect that the partial failure of this novel, at the end, results from MacLennan's failure to be true to his own deepest insight, as to the value of life in the flesh as well as in the spirit. He finds himself unable to rest with a literature of truth, such as the great Russian literature which he admires, and unable to rest with the metaphorical expression of truth veiled in the flesh of his characters, characters such as Josephine Martell and Jerome who represent love incarnate and who make the major portions of this novel great. MacLennan's intellectualism-cum-mysticism makes him turn from this to a "literature of understanding," and a didactic effort to pin down the truth in words. His words are vague ones, such as "the pattern of our lives and fates," "the mystery surrounding us," or "the mystery which our ancestors confidently called God," but this only makes the matter worse. Vague words are a poor substitute for an evocation of the material world which shows that world so thoroughly penetrated by spirit that the dichotomy disappears.

NOTES

1. See Peter Buitenhuis, *Hugh MacLennan* (Toronto: Forum House, 1969), pp. 56-7. Cf. Robert H. Cockburn, *The Novels of Hugh MacLennan* (Montreal: Harvest House, 1969), p. 112: "George . . . is not the sort toward whom a reader is attracted – not unless he outgrows his weakness and redeems himself in our eyes. George never quite succeeds." Cockburn believes that MacLennan has purposely made George "weak" because this is MacLennan's conception of Everyman. Cockburn's repeated insistence that George is "not the sort of man one chooses to identify with" (p. 114) seriously underestimates the quiet strength which we see slowly maturing in the narrator.

2. Buitenhuis, *Hugh MacLennan*, pp. 56-7.

3. Cf. Cockburn, *The Novels of Hugh MacLennan*, p. 120: "Jerome is impossible to believe in and in his own way he bids fair to be more unreal than Catherine. His life is that of a Hollywood hero. . . ." The Bethune biography, however, shows us an actual man every whit as dynamic and multifaceted as MacLennan's Jerome Martell.

4. This quotation from Rilke forms the epigraph and theme of *Two Solitudes*, where marriage supplies a national as well as a personal solution

to separation. *Return of the Sphinx*, demonstrating once again MacLennan's belief in Canada's destiny as a united nation with two main cultures, employs marriage (or the permanent love of two individuals who yet retain their own identity) as an archetypal metaphor for the ideal relationship between cultures or individuals.

5. Hugh MacLennan, "The Story of a Novel," *Masks of Fiction*, NCL 02 (Toronto: McClelland and Stewart, 1961), p. 37.

6. Buitenhuis, *Hugh MacLennan*, p. 64.

10 THE GOOD LAND

A good land. We find the phrase and its variations recurring constantly in MacLennan's sixth novel, *Return of the Sphinx*, where Canada and Constance, the hero's lost wife, are identified with one another and with the goodness of life. And conversely, the senseless brutality of revolution and war is depicted as a death force, the incarnation of the demonic or Sphinx-element in man. Once again, MacLennan's theme is life against death.

This conflict underlies all of MacLennan's fiction. In *The Sphinx*, however, it is more prominent, and operates as a basic structural principle. It is this theme which unifies the novel, defining the experience of the characters and controlling the motifs and patterns of imagery. The characters can be grouped according to their sympathetic alignment with or antagonism towards life. In Hollywood terms, we have the Good Guys and the Bad Guys: on the one hand, Alan Ainslie, his wife Constance, his daughter Chantal, his best friend Gabriel Fleury, and the Provenchers, a large French-Canadian rural family; and on the other, the death-seekers – Daniel, Clarisse and Latendresse. Marielle, mother of Clarisse, is a special case. MacLennan's final denunciation of her is very similar to the strange acceptance-rejection treatment accorded Kathleen in *Two Solitudes*.

It is paradoxical that a novel the narrative of which is based upon a specific country at a particular and critical point in its history (the separatist crisis of the sixties in Quebec) is at the same time the most traditional of MacLennan's novels to date. This novel draws heavily upon the archetypal patterns and figures common to Western literature since Greek drama and poetry in the pre-Christian era. There is the orphan figure, a bewildered child-man, spiritually adrift and wandering in a violent age. There is the father who has been murdered or badly deformed; the generation conflict between father and son; the eternally faithful wife; the incest motif. Oedipus and Odysseus? Of course. Freudian theories? Very frequently. But these are catch names, and we are tired of conjuring with them. Certainly these patterns (of wandering, of homelessness and so on) are present in *The Sphinx*, as George Woodcock emphasizes in connection with all MacLennan's fiction. But why insist that the novel is based upon Homer's *Odyssey*? The experiences and images associated with these archetypal or conventional patterns are part of Western literature from its earliest beginnings, and part of our human heritage or psychic birthright.

The mythic patterns in *The Sphinx* are far too frequent to be accidental. The experience of every one of the major characters is based upon them, and the life-against-death theme is structured largely in terms of these patterns. The characters who have seen their father murdered or deformed include Daniel and Chantal (Ainslie's face has been badly scarred on one side in the war), Ainslie, Bulstrode, Gabriel, Marielle. The external disfigurement represents the psychic scars inflicted by the violence in which they have been unwillingly involved. Nearly all of the characters have lost one or both parents through violent means. The orphan figure typifies (as MacLennan tells us plainly, here as in his earlier fiction) every human being in the post-war twentieth century, "modern man living as a human exile among abstractions." (*RS* 187) Science, technology and the System have made orphans of us all; or, to take a key image from *The Watch That Ends the Night*, have set us adrift on an ocean in a canoe with a hurricane rising.

Paul Tallard's loss of both parents, in *Two Solitudes*, is invested with the same meaning. Paul tells Heather that *The Odyssey* is a universal story, applicable on many levels: "Science and war – and God knows what else – have uprooted us and the whole world is roaming. Its mind is roaming, Heather. Its mind is going mad trying to find a new place to live. . . . I feel it – right here in myself. I've been living in the waiting room of a railway station." Since Paul is specifically identified with "the new Canada," the modern Canadian is depicted in both *Two Solitudes* and *The Sphinx* as an exile in a culture which is essentially alien to the human spirit.

The Canadian land occurs in MacLennan's earlier work as an apocalyptic image of goodness and life. The land is obviously "in the blood," not only of the Quebec habitant but also of MacLennan. In *Two Solitudes*, Athanase Tallard tells Captain Yardley that

French-Canadians feel towards the land as do Europeans. They love it, and look after it better than they look after themselves. The parishioners of Saint-Marc-des-Erables regard the proposed factory and its concomitant urban and technological growth as something leprous or cancerous on the face of the good land. Yardley agrees with Tallard that it is *good* land; he is sensitive to its beauty, and the tossing of bare trees in the wind reminds him of the beauty he has seen in the depths of clear waters. The Blanchard family plays a role here similar to that of the Provenchers in *The Sphinx*. Blanchard has worked Tallard land for twenty-five years and knows it to be good. We are told that an impression of well-being, "almost of goodness," emanates from Blanchard along with the smell of stable and sweat. As in *The Sphinx*, the land and those who love it are as one, and part of Athanase Tallard's tragedy lies in his isolation from his inherited land and its people.

In his introductory Note to *Each Man's Son*, MacLennan speaks of loving an island, and of feeling towards it as one can towards a woman. It seems apparent that, by the sixties, he feels this way not just towards Cape Breton but towards all of Canada. He has always been an ardent nationalist from the time of his first published novel. But perhaps his original love for his own land has been heightened even further by what Carl Klinck refers to as "the ground-swell of cultural nationalism," which began to get rolling in the fifties. *And* by the jealous fear (we may consider the sexual analogy here, since MacLennan thinks of the land as feminine) that his beloved country may be lost to an economically aggressive neighbour.

Speaking in Montreal, on May 14, 1971, to a group concerned with the survival of Canada as an independent nation, MacLennan described Canada as "curiously feminine." He made the same point, that the Canadian nation is feminine, earlier, in an essay, "The Canadian Character." (*CC* 5) In *Two Solitudes*, Dennis Morey compares the land around Winnipeg to "a great majestic bowl with the earth flat beneath it. Sky the giver, earth the accepter. Male and female." In *The Sphinx*, the good land of Canada is the Magna Mater, both wife and mother, identified with joy and goodness, with all things desirable which make life worth living. Alan Ainslie's personal quest is *one* with his country's destiny. He regards its possible dissolution, especially through violent means, as a personal death, whereas his marriage into an ancient French-Canadian family, like the marriage of Paul and Heather in *Two Solitudes*, symbolizes the marriage of what Ainslie sees as the two dominant cultures of Canada. This loving relationship is imaged by the land itself, "lake and forest married in perfect silence."

Northrop Frye, writing of the narrative tradition in English-Canadian poetry, notes that the mindless, amoral and impersonal aspect of the Canadian wilderness has caught the imagination of many Canadian poets. He suggests that the Canadian landscape and experience "demand" a tragic resolution. MacLennan has given us a glimpse of this forbidding landscape in Heather's description of the vastness of a Laurentian scene – "the sense of the cold wind stretching so many hundreds of miles to the north of it, through ice and tundra and desolation." Unlike the narrative tradition in much of English-Canadian poetry, however, MacLennan most frequently uses the vast land ("too vast even for fools to ruin all of it") as a symbol of hope and joy. In *The Watch That Ends the Night*, Catherine's joy in being alive, despite pain, is reflected in the joyful colours of her paintings. George remarks that these gay colours are unusual in paintings of Canada, a land "which so many painters see as sombre except in the fall." He approves. After George accepts that Catherine must live her own death, and accepts the gifts of life with grateful joy, he realizes that spring is beginning and that spring is nowhere more beautiful "than in this northern land where it comes when there is still snow." At peace within himself, George is reborn like the land around him. MacLennan depicts the Canadian landscape as comforting, joyous, good. It is through the land and the possibilities inherent in it that *Return of the Sphinx* drives towards a comic or happy resolution.

The good land and the good marriage are revealed through archetypal or apocalyptic metaphors identified with the social goals of human desire: the well-tended garden, the wild-flowering open spaces, the happy family, and the larger social unit, the ideal city or community. Archetypal imagery is based upon a dialectic of desire and repugnance. Thus, when the vision is distorted by bitterness and despair, the good land is seen as demonic, abhorrent. At the end of Part One, when Ainslie is alone in Montreal at 3:00 in the morning, with his world collapsing around him, the beloved country appears as nothing but a barren wilderness with a few ant-hills, where foolish ants believe that they possess and control the vast land from their little heaps.

Ainslie's black vision at this juncture is like that of Dostoevski's Anna Karenina shortly before her suicide, when all naturally good things appear to her as their opposites: when children are hideous and lovers repulsive, when all relationships are based only upon hatred and issue only in suffering. These demonic visions may be compared with the experience of Ainslie's foster father in *Each Man's Son*. In Chapter Twenty-six of this earlier novel, Daniel Ainslie faces the prospect of losing the child he has come to love; realizing the crippling fear in which he has lived until then, he contemplates "a world without purpose, without meaning, without intelligence."

Like Daniel, Alan Ainslie experiences the abyss of despair, the existential *angst* described so poignantly by Tillich and Kierkegaard as the loss of hopes and ideals, the facing of meaninglessness. This is more bitter than death itself: "The idea came to him that he had no work that mattered any more, no love that mattered any more, no hope that mattered any more." (*RS* 164) The idea came to him that his journey was over and had brought him to a dead end rather than to the desired goal. His adult crisis merges with the crisis he had experienced as a boy. Then, he witnessed the violent death of his beloved mother; now he faces the death of his hopes for his country, Canada. It is at this point that he sees the land as a wilderness with anthills.

Gabriel Fleury, whose career sums up the history of two generations and the end of the era of British and French colonial empires, fears that the youthful Canada, potentially a great nation, may be *stillborn*. He fears that history is once more on the point of hunting him down or turning him into a homeless man adrift in a dying country. Death dominates the mood of Part One's short third chapter, where the death of empires and cultures is imaged in the death dance of a trillion summer-swarming insects.

Chantal sees her father's dedication to Canada as a misplaced ideal, a misguided Pilgrim's Progress. Out of the bitterness born of her knowledge of her father's suffering and his apparent ineffectiveness in the current political hassles, she sardonically describes Canada as a perverted City of God, a demonic city where greed brings rewards and true service, suffering and punishment. Gabriel rebukes her for her depreciation of Canada, referring to the national habit of self-depreciation, and quoting her father's wartime prophecy: "That funny country I come from, if she can accept her own nature and live with it, is going to become priceless to mankind." (*RS* 43–4) Gabriel's attitude towards Canada is governed throughout by his tremendous respect for Ainslie's judgement.

The entire context of the novel convinces one that Ainslie's attitude towards the country is that of MacLennan himself. Chantal, in a passing mood, mocks the progress of the pilgrim, mocks the puritan search for the holy community, and the puritan's reforming activism which seeks to establish the City of God upon earth. But Ainslie never mocks this goal, although he may despair of its realization. Nor does the author, if one takes MacLennan's views to be those embodied in the novel as a whole. Ainslie's dedication to his country is essentially religious and, in terms of the historic definition we have established for the word, Puritan.

A mystique surrounds Ainslie's love and reverence for his country, this potential Zion. His feeling for Canada is the love of a man for child, wife, parents; the quixotic love of a medieval knight for his lady; and the mystical love of a religious soul for God. In the German prison camp, Ainslie has spoken to Gabriel of his vast land whose lakes and deltas and prairie sloughs he has looked upon with awe, while wondering if her people would ever become worthy of her. (This idea is a variation on Ainslie's conviction that each country must *earn* its way into civilization. Canada's inhabitants must earn their way into true citizenship, as it were.) Gabriel understands that he loves the land "as some people love the idea of growth in a child." Many politicians regard the country as an *object* to be manipulated for their own gain, but Ainslie relates to it as to a beloved *person*. Such a relationship is essentially religious, as Martin Buber reminds us in *I and Thou*.

Ainslie, like MacLennan's earlier heroes, is the quintessential Puritan: serious, intellectual, hard-working, moral-*cum*-mystical (without, in MacLennan's humanistic version, adhering to any formal religious tradition), and dedicated to promoting the good of the human community as he sees it. Ainslie has aided his country through war service, publishing, and service in the federal government. He tells Joe Lacombe that he is, by nature, a religious man. Ainslie is repeatedly called "saintly," and while his religious zeal is sometimes termed naïve or quixotic, it is also clearly intended to compel our admiration and respect. The youths who interview Ainslie consider him naïve but sincere. Tarnley calls him an exceptional man, a *chevalier*, and his hostile son Daniel grants that his father would give his life for Confederation.

Chantal emphasizes that her father's idealism has been slowly tempered by bitter realities. By frequent comments on Ainslie's *naïveté,* and by making Ainslie laugh at Tarnley's naïve hope for social rebirth through a select community of scholars, MacLennan intends to dissociate himself from Ainslie's shortcomings in this regard. One cannot help feeling that the dissociation is only partly successful, that the morally serious puritan in Ainslie is by no means dead, and that Ainslie's character is very close to that of his creator. Constance is the perfect complement to Ainslie. Since she supplies what he lacks and needs, their marriage suggests, among other things, that the French and Anglo-Saxon natures are naturally complementary. Constance is a more idealized version of Catherine Martell. The two women are very similar, but we see less of Constance. Her close identification with the good land and the symbolic overtones of the way in which she is killed tend to project her in a larger-than-life, or mythical, role. Constance is the eternal woman, earthy yet spiritual, with the joyous gaiety that Ainslie lacks. Just as his adult experience of desolation merges with his childhood crisis and the murder of his mother, so the happiness of one long-remembered afternoon as a child on a beach with his mother merges with the consummation of his love for Catherine. The paragraph in *The Sphinx* describing the boy and his mother on a lonely beach is taken from *Each Man's Son*. It consciously echoes the exact phrasing of the earlier novel. The homecoming, which had been joyfully anticipated by the boy on the beach and rudely shattered by Archie MacNeil's return, is fulfilled for Ainslie in his relationship with Constance: "The scene had come back to him on the first night he had loved Constance, and the whole promontory had taken off and swung up into the sky, turned itself upside down and fallen and become Constance herself, and the high clouds of childhood had rested still." (*RS* 115) Canada and Constance thus play a single role in the novel, imaging the goal of Ainslie's quest, his spiritual home. With the death of Constance, Ainslie's final homecoming is to the land, "too vast even for fools to ruin all of it."

The attempted assassination of his country by revolution is as brutally senseless as the action of the runaway truck which kills Constance.[1] MacLennan sees war and revolution as a neurotic urge to self-destruction. Marielle tells Daniel to change his dreams or they will destroy him: "You are afraid of loving a woman, and if a man fears that, then it is very natural for him to talk and dream about bombs and war." (*RS* 153) Ainslie tells his son that the Quebec revolutionary movement is simply a wave in the age-old flow of history. The Sphinx represents the demonic, destructive element in both man and his world.[2] This death-wish opposes man's desire for life and joy; the monstrous nature of the image suggests a non-human force within human nature. Thus the key images which contain the novel's theme of life against death are the apocalyptic images of a happy marriage and a fruitful land, and the demonic image of an impersonal monstrous violence.

Violence is also condemned by MacLennan in his novels of the fifties, *The Watch That Ends the Night* and *Each Man's Son*. Jerome Martell defines the ultimate evil as cruelty. Both Jerome and Alan Ainslie are child witnesses to the brutal murders of their mothers. These incidents serve as archetypes, in their respective novels, of the violence which MacLennan abhors. In *The Sphinx*, war and revolution are the archetypal forms of this death-urge, and the most powerful descriptive passages in the novel are those depicting violent destruction: the death of Constance, the hurricane at sea, the attack on the *Jean Bart* at Casablanca. MacLennan has always been at his best in descriptive passages of this type, and no one who has read *Barometer Rising* will ever forget the magnificent description of the explosion of the *Mont Blanc* in Halifax harbour. In *Barometer Rising*, however, the violence eventually becomes a force for good. It serves a constructive purpose by shattering the old rigid social hierarchies and the colonial mentality which had bound the country in a subservient role. Similarly, the violent energy of old John Knox Cameron in *The Precipice* is seen as a form of the life-force, as is the storm which rages round the Cameron house as Lucy makes her decision to marry Stephen. But in *The Sphinx* there is no hint that violence could possibly be a force for good.

World War I is presented (through Gabriel's point of view, blended with that of the omniscient narrator) as the time when the present situation really began: "What had started then was surely *the rebirth of a kind of man who had perished two thousand years ago*, a man who knew there was no escape from his own nature into religion or politics or science or even into his own skill [italics mine]." (*RS* 170) The experience suggested by the title of Ainslie's book, *Death of a Victorian*, is obviously that of the liberal optimist of the nineteenth and early twentieth centuries. (Cohen calls it the Breavman ethic.) This optimism concerning human nature and society was shattered in World War I. MacLennan's sentence implies that the pre-Christian kind of man reborn through twentieth-century violence harbours no illusions about his perfectibility, and no illusions about the possibility of evading the demonic urges which periodically erupt in him. It implies, further, that for nineteen centuries Christianity had encouraged the illusion of man's perfectibility, but the illusion had to be discarded as such after the brutal realities of World War I.

It was a strange view that the Victorians held, both of history and of Christianity. History, among other things, is a record of unending wars and senseless violence. The Victorians, convinced that "civilized" and educated men do not resort to violence, had succeeded in shutting their eyes to the facts of history, until their illusions were shattered by the war. The Christian religion has never encouraged man to believe he could escape from his own nature into religion or politics or any other human sphere – but the Victorians had somehow persuaded themselves that it had. The myth of human perfectibility and moral progress dies hard.

Canada's October Crisis of 1970 had a psychological effect somewhat similar, on a smaller scale, to that of World War I. It marked an end to innocence. No longer could we pretend that there might be revolutionary violence in Latin America or the Far East but *not here*, not in Canada. As MacLennan emphasizes in *Return of the Sphinx*, violence is endemic throughout the world today. The October Revolution confirmed many of the points which he makes in this novel concerning the nature of the revolutionary struggle.

"Revolutionaries are dead men on furlough." The separatist Latendresse draws "much comfort" from this remark of Lenin's. Cold comfort, indeed, but Latendresse is a man of deadly cold. Lenin's remark sums up MacLennan's view of the revolutionaries and defines the imagistic pattern of coldness used in connection with them: grey, glacial coldness, completely void of human feelings. Daniel notes that Latendresse is much older, psychically, than the others. The novel suggests that he is as old as death itself. When Latendresse describes revolutionary technique as the art of getting the car to the crest of the hill so that the impersonal force of gravity will act to reinforce the demonic in man, we are reminded of the manner of Constance's death. Daniel begins to realize his latent hostility towards Latendresse, from whom people recoil as from a walking corpse.

Daniel shares, to a certain extent, the characteristics of Latendresse, while being a more complex and ambivalent figure. Torn by divided loyalties, Daniel oscillates between separatist sympathies and the values embodied in his parents and Clarisse's mother Marielle. Clarisse is a female version of Latendresse. A minor figure, she provides an echo of the death motif established through Latendresse and Daniel, and serves as a foil for Marielle's warmth. Marielle tells Daniel that Clarisse hates men and herself, and that she has been hostile ever since she was a baby.

MacLennan depicts the revolutionaries as puritan, by the definition established in his early novels: guilt, combined with fear and the rejection of the pleasures of life, tends to become the rejection of life itself.³ All revolutions, Ainslie informs Bulstrode, have neurotic roots. MacLennan sees the revolutionary as a psychopath, obsessed with the idea of the enemy, fearful of sex, and bent upon self-destruction. The application of the label "puritan" to this type of personality casts a further light on his earlier novels where the attack on puritanism is a constant theme. This interpretation of the revolutionary emerges clearly from Daniel's talk with Marielle in Chapter Nine of Book One. Speaking of Clarisse's neuroses, of her self-willed ignorance and her basic hostility, Marielle says that all North Americans are puritans, and "don't even guess" what it does to them. She attempts to lead Daniel to realize his own fear of being a man and loving a woman.

When Daniel disagrees with her condemnation of Latendresse, she proceeds to tell him the story of her father's death at Casablanca aboard the *Jean Bart*. Marielle, like Gabriel Fleury and Daniel's father, and unlike Daniel himself, has seen and lived with the violence of war. In line with MacLennan's thesis that the revolutionaries refuse to face history, Daniel has always shunned war stories as boring. By remaining ignorant of the horrors of war at close hand, he can continue to see violence as a thing of glory and glamour. Marielle ends that. She ends it with her description of the Americans washing the remains of her father and his men out of the turret with hoses; she ends it with the story of her giving herself to a young American lieutenant for two dozen tins of Spam and half a dozen cartons of cigarettes which could be sold for more food. A similarly horrifying description of the remains of bodies being washed out with hoses forms the basis of one of Randall Jarrell's poems. MacLennan uses a slight variant a few pages later in connection with the murder of Ainslie's mother, "the gentle woman, flushed out of the world like water swirling down a drain when the plug has been pulled." The images imply that the destructive forces in man merge with the destructive force in the instruments which man fashions through his technology.

Patterns of association in the novel connect the demonic Sphinx not only with the destruction in revolution and war but also with a distorted worship of technology and efficiency in a consumer-oriented society. Many passages parallel the attack mounted upon *la technic* by the French lay theologian Jacques Ellul. Technique, as Ellul points out, tends to become a self-justifying and all-inclusive monster, an inhuman force which subordinates the spiritual to the material. In the process, the end becomes that which furthers the means.[4]

Latent in MacLennan's novel is the Ellulian concept that the subordination of the spiritual to the technical is *the* revolution of our day. As Tarnley puts it, "the controllers are controlled by the things they control." The means take over the ends, the sorcerer's apprentice is no longer subservient, and once-controlled things become as uncontrollable as the runaway truck which snuffs out Constance's life. Gabriel's divorced wife believes in a "planned society," where the road to paradise is via correct technique.[5] Less sanguine, Gabriel characterizes the Anglo-Saxon attitude as one which regards life as a series of problems to be solved by intelligent management. In the eighth chapter, Latendresse voices the same type of criticism, and blames the Anglo-Saxon System for turning people into a producing and consuming machine while ignoring the fact that this "destroys their meaning." The doggerel composed by Ainslie as he faces the apparent failure of his efforts to further the cause of national unity neatly pinpoints the self-destructive aspect of man's technique: "It's not the earth you've hit, / It's yourself, you shit! / Your computer has made a blunder."

Explosive devices depend upon technique. More important, the entire technique of managing a revolution has evolved into a science, as Latendresse points out to Daniel. Thus the runaway truck (technique gone wild) which destroys Ainslie's family life is essentially one with the destructive forces at work in a technological society, and one with the death-wish of the revolutionaries. MacLennan's demonic or Sphinx imagery is remarkably unified and interrelated.

Daniel Ainslie, after reading the story of his grandfather's last fight and his insane murder of Mollie, has a demonic vision of mankind as a swarm of animated automatons. Sex is reduced to a relationship between robots, and the child born of these robots is totally subject to deterministic forces. Daniel's waking nightmare corresponds to Ainslie's tortured vision of Canada as a wilderness with anthills, a space without meaning or value.

MacLennan's earlier novels also contain attacks on *la technic*, connecting it with the materialism of North American culture as well as with the means of waging war. In *Two Solitudes*, the power dam, which will turn the parish of Saint-Marc into a factory town, is termed inevitable: "science was bound to crack the shell of Quebec sooner or later." At times MacLennan seems as ambivalent towards this development as Athanase Tallard, whose reason puts him "on the side of science," and whose emotions pull him towards faith and the soil; as ambivalent as Paul Tallard, who tells Heather he is sorry that he couldn't cope with science in the university, since "science is the new theology." The context does not suggest irony. Similarly in " 'Help Thou Mine Unbelief,' " an essay written at about the same time as *Two Solitudes*, MacLennan writes that science has shattered the traditional Christian theology, and that a new theology must be reconstructed suited to "an age dominated by science among the educated and by industrialism among the masses." (*CC* 145) Neither here, nor in "A Second Look," added as a postscript to this essay for the published collection, does MacLennan imply that science is not to be trusted. Rather, he looks to science to produce the new theology for modern man: "it is for science to formulate in intelligible terms the concepts of God-as-purpose and God-as-origin. If it fails to do so, modern man will lack religion in exact proportion to the extent of his education. Mystical interpretation of these concepts of God no longer touches the scientifically trained." (*CC* 155)

At other times, however, MacLennan's attack on technology is unambiguous. Daphne's husband Noel is the man of technique, a "new species of human being" whom MacLennan clearly abhors. The life of Marius, Tallard's neurotically unhappy son, is described as a reflection of the tragedy of the transition to the new way of life which is being forced upon everyone by science and technology. Most damning is the description of the machine as standing *behind Hitler,* transforming men into robots dedicated solely to efficiency and to efficient destruction. (*TS* 318)

We have noted that the characters in *Return of the Sphinx* fall naturally into two camps in connection with the theme of life against death. Marielle is the exception. In the first book Marielle is identified with those who are on the side of life. It is largely through her discussion with Daniel that MacLennan establishes his view of revolutionaries as neurotic personalities bent on destroying both others and themselves. Marielle, in this scene, is archetypal woman, "the enormous unknown," inviting Daniel to enter life through love: "When the truth can be so good, why do we resist it?" Her calm and erect presence has already reminded Daniel of his mother and of her life-giving security. He describes his father as being perfectly *safe* so long as his mother was alive.

Daniel responds to Marielle's appeal to love. On the following day, he thinks that she "had surely delivered him from himself." (*RS* 196) From his deathly self. Thus Marielle, in Book One and Intermezzo, is the non-puritan spokesman for life. The entire context of the first two-thirds of the novel – the handling of narrative and characterization and images – indicates that MacLennan approves of her relationship with Daniel. Daniel's thought that Marielle resembles his mother is especially significant, because of the mythical role played by Constance, her identification with the good land and with the goal of life. After making love to Marielle, Daniel no longer feels hostile towards and in competition with his father. And Marielle is depicted as loving Daniel in a total, personal way, rather than being simply concerned with sexual gratification.

Why then does MacLennan describe their love-making by scientific images of explosions and chain-reactions, images which recall the destructive violence of Marielle's Casablanca story? Is it a conscious effort to oppose the explosive force of life to that of death? Or is MacLennan using scientific terms to avoid more intimate descriptions which a puritan censor in his own consciousness forbids? The critics are fond of pointing out, in recent years, that MacLennan handles many of the love scenes in his fiction with an embarrassed awkwardness. Obviously MacLennan has no desire to write the kind of clinical descriptions of the sexual act which are found in many novels of the sixties. I think that he *is*, at times, capable of writing about love in a way that suggests both sensitivity and passion. George Woodcock mocks the ending scene in *Barometer Rising* for its "stock clichés of romanticist fiction – tears, moonlight, sudden smiles, fingers touching temples and wind rising in the forest."[6] But I find effective an earlier love scene in this novel, where Neil and Penny consummate their love in a room fragrant with full-blown peonies.

What strikes one as strange is not so much MacLennan's uneasiness in the handling of love scenes as his rejection, loud and clear, of a character with whom he has previously led us to identify sympathetically. He has done this in *Two Solitudes* with Kathleen. She is treated sympathetically in Part One, and is credited with giving her son, Paul, security and joy, and with giving Athanase Tallard the will to live, by sleeping with him on the night of the death of his first wife. MacLennan stresses her earthy gentleness and innocence here, only to damn her in the second part as lazy, uncaring, irresponsible, and sensuous in a way that the author pictures as undesirable.

His treatment of Marielle in *Return of the Sphinx* is very similar. After associating her with Constance in Book One, and crediting her with helping Daniel to understand and overcome his destructive hostility, Marielle is rejected in Chapter Nine of Book Two, where

Ainslie discovers her and Daniel together in his apartment. She is rejected here quite unambiguously as an immoral and shameful woman. We should ask ourselves how her motives, in thus attempting to overcome Daniel's basic antagonism to life, differ from those of the male relative who first introduced Constance to sex as a life-giving art? Or do they differ? And if not, why the pattern of approval *first*, and rejection *second*? One is driven to conclude that MacLennan's own feelings, if not his reason, are still opposed towards sex outside a permanent marriage-type relationship.

A musical analogy serves best to describe this novel's structure. The theme, life against death, is played and replayed with subtle variations through the experiences of different characters and by means of a pattern of imagery. One critic, while acknowledging that MacLennan's fiction is always strongly thematic, remains blind to this orchestral structure and criticizes the plot for "meandering" and the flashbacks as "digressive."[7] Another critic objects to "multiple narrative centres," instead of the single narrative voice of *The Watch That Ends the Night.*[8] We should remember that, the novels of Henry James and Joseph Conrad notwithstanding, there is nothing *inherently* superior in the technique of the single narrative voice.

Except for its Epilogue, *Return of the Sphinx* takes place in eight days, like *Barometer Rising*. The traumatic week when Ainslie, Minister of Cultural Affairs, is betrayed by the political and revolutionary acts of his son falls within the year when his wife has been killed by a runaway truck. This year is part of a traumatic century in which the senseless violence of two world wars has ended the rational optimism which Ainslie terms "Victorian": "All the ideas that had guided and inspired Ainslie's life – socialism, education, the faith that science and prosperity would improve man's life, even the new psychology which everyone so glibly talked – the best he could say now of any of these hopes was that they had foundered in the ancient ocean of human nature." (*RS* 74–5)

In childhood, Gabriel Fleury has seen war turn his father into a mangled, wheezing wreck; and still his family thirsted for another boy to sacrifice upon the altar of the monstrous god of war. The Sphinx-pattern of mindless destruction is built orchestrally. The variations include the deaths of Constance, of Gabriel's father, of Marielle's father, of Ainslie's gentle mother. There is the fearful storm at sea, which Ainslie has experienced on a freighter in his youth and recalls during the "hurricane weather" of Montreal during the sixties. The Sphinx-mood is caught in the refrain "Run, run, run till you die, / fox at your heels and crow in the sky." This demonic version of the Journey turns the quest for the meaning of life into a dead end, a blank wall, a trap. And this is exactly the way Ainslie feels at 3:00 in the morning, soon after he has learned of Daniel's part in the riot. At the beginning of the Epilogue, Ainslie has resigned his portfolio, denounced the period in which he lives as a "sick epoch," told his son to leave their house and go his own way, and rejected as naïve Tarnley's suggestion that Ainslie become the head of a small and select liberal arts college which might function as a moral and intellectual refuge, like the European monasteries in the Dark Ages. "The walls of his life and meaning dissolved around him": psychically, Ainslie has died, like Jerome Martell in his solitary prison confinement.

Life against death. The tight time scheme which has held the novel until this point is now loosened. As Ainslie journeys across Canada from coast to coast, summer flows into early autumn and the prairie wheat begins to turn to gold. The mood is one of joy, peace, thankfulness; of an overflowing cup filled by a beneficent deity: "now thank we all our God." As Ainslie leaves the Provencher wedding party, his mind is filled with images of the land, the good land, "lake and forest married in perfect silence." He joyfully anticipates the wedding of Gabriel and Chantal. And he feels the living presence of his wife Constance. The Epilogue, which has begun with death, ends as an epithalamium. Ainslie's mood is very similar to that of George Stewart at the ending of *The Watch*, but without the references to shadows and transparency which marred the closing chapters of that novel.[9] Three human marriages mingle in his thoughts with the marriage of lake and forest, land and sky. Ainslie accepts "this loveliness" with gratitude, joy and the confidence that it will endure.

NOTES

1. Cf. Alec Lucas, *Hugh MacLennan* (Toronto: McClelland and Stewart, 1970), p. 20: "The runaway truck that killed Alan Ainslie's wife and destroyed his happy marriage also signifies what the rapid modernization of Quebec has meant to the old relationship between the two cultures of the province."

2. Cf. Hugh MacLennan, "Murder of Truth . . . murder of people," *The Gazette*, Montreal, November 21, 1970, p. 8: "The title of this novel came to me exactly one minute after I wrote the last line. Clearly it goes back to the Oedipus legend on the Sphinx which made cities sick, tore families asunder, set sons against fathers and daughters against mothers, resulting in parricides and infanticides in pre-historic times." In the same article, MacLennan describes the older separatist Latendresse as "Daniel's evil genius."

3. See E. J. Hobsbawm, "Revolution is Puritan," in *The New Eroticism: Theories, Vogues and Canons*, ed. Philip Nobile (New York: Random House, 1970), p. 38: "There *is*, I am bound to note with a little regret, a persistent affinity between revolution and puritanism. I can think of no well-established organized revolutionary movement or regime which has not developed marked puritan tendencies."

4. See Jacques Ellul, *The Technological Society* (New York: Vintage, 1964), *passim*, and *The Presence of the Kingdom* (New York: Seabury, 1967), especially Chapter 3, "The End and the Means."

5. It is interesting to note, in connection with MacLennan's frequent use of marriage as an apocalyptic image or archetypal metaphor, identified with all things desirable, that he often attributes undesirable attitudes to the divorced mates of his fictional characters. In *The Precipice*, Joyce, Lassiter's ex-wife, is depicted as cold and unfeeling, in contrast to Lucy's warmth. In *The Sphinx*, the attitude of Gabriel's ex-wife is obviously the opposite to MacLennan's.

6. George Woodcock, "A Nation's Odyssey," *Odysseus Ever Returning*, NCL 71 (Toronto: McClelland and Stewart, 1970), p. 15.

7. Robert H. Cockburn, *The Novels of Hugh MacLennan* (Montreal: Harvest House, 1969), pp. 135, 136, 140.

8. Peter Buitenhuis, *Hugh MacLennan* (Toronto: Forum House, 1969), p. 69.

9. Cf. Buitenhuis, p. 71: "The land, then, is the great reconciler and the great resolver for all problems of its people. . . . Nevertheless, I cannot help feeling that the overarching land and this marriage is an insufficient resolution for a story which ends with a son in jail and a father's career in ruins . . . the vision of reconciliation seems unearned."

11 RETURN OF THE MORALIST

C.S. Lewis represents the devil as rejoicing in the current low repute of the word "puritanism." Screwtape and his fellow devils claim to have rescued thousands of humans from temperance, chastity and sobriety, by means of debasing this word.[1] Lewis is suggesting, whimsically but with considerable truth, that it is the devil's work to allow the connotations of the word "puritan" to be entirely negative and undesirable. I agree. The sympathetic treatment of the Roundheads in Ken Hughes' 1971 movie, "Cromwell," indicates that the word is being currently reevaluated and will no longer serve as a catch-all for whatever the writer happens to dislike.

In our discussion in Chapter Two, of the atypical phenomenon of group sex, the point is made that Canada is basically a religious country: religious, moral, reformist in its basic drives. The moral preoccupations we have been examining in the work of two such apparently different Canadian novelists as MacLennan and Cohen should go far towards establishing this point. This is a part, and a significant part, of that elusive and protean creature, the Canadian identity. Some may quarrel with the particular words chosen to connote our shared experience. In his preface to *The Bush Garden: Essays on the Canadian Imagination*, Northrop Frye distinguishes between cultural or imaginative *identity* and political *unity*. He sees Canada as a pluralistic society which seeks to maintain a dialectical tension between the political sense of national unity and the imaginative sense nurtured in particular localities. While emphasizing the regional element in "identity," Frye acknowledges that there are imaginative forms which are common to the whole country.[2]

I suggest that one important element in these "containing imaginative forms," forms which are common to the experience of many

Canadians, is the Puritan ethic. Puritanism is the traditional moral conscience and consciousness which marks Canadian culture and has played a primary role in the Canadian imagination. Hugh Mac-Lennan was brought up in Nova Scotia, while I am a native of Toronto. Yet MacLennan's thought-world or cultural heritage is thoroughly familiar to me and, reading his novels, I find myself an insider to most of the attitudes and problems found in his fictional situations. Broughton and Grenville, Halifax and Montreal, Toronto, Ottawa and Winnipeg are blood brothers under the skin. Puritanism has marked Canadians of many different religious faiths. It has marked them through its rationalism and its moral idealism; marked them, too, by the deliberate reaction which its extreme forms have provoked. In the last few decades we have been witnessing this re-action in the form of a swing to moral permissiveness.

It may be argued that this religious idealism is not peculiar to Canada. Obviously it is not an exclusively Canadian characteristic. We are speaking in terms of the *prominence* of its role in the life of the people as a whole. On the North American continent Puritanism began in New England. But by the eighteenth and nineteenth centuries it had become a much less significant part of the American national ethos, whereas the major immigrations to Canada during this time (Scots, Loyalists, etc.) had strengthened the hold of Puritanism on the Canadian imagination.[3] One of Max Ferguson's recent radio skits sets Canadian Cabinet minister Mitchell Sharp in Washington talking with some wealthy Texans.[4] Sharp wants to keep on discussing the problems without stopping for lunch (Puritan self-discipline, moralism and appetite for work). The Texans have no intention of missing lunch, and suggest they draw to decide who pays for it. The Canadian Minister would like to eat in the government cafeteria (frugality, and Puritan abstemiousness with regard to food), but the Texans have ordered a mass of delicacies sent in from all over the world. We laugh – but doesn't the shoe fit? Would it have made any sense if the characteristics had been reversed? (And guess who loses the draw and gets the bill.)

Diffidence is a Canadian characteristic, and Cohen has been praised as being "so Canadian, a little tentative, kind of droll and self-depreciating."[5] The diffidence of many Canadians is such that a writer must argue not only that certain factors or characteristics are part of the Canadian identity, but that such an identity does in fact exist. Ronald Sutherland's studies of the themes common to the literature of English and French Canada point to an underlying unity in the values held by many diverse Canadian groups – United

Empire Loyalists, Scots, French-Canadians and others. This subject is a study in itself, as Sutherland's work demonstrates, and cannot be explored further here.[6] But whether we call it a "national mystique," with Sutherland, or "containing imaginative forms," or simply shared attitudes and experiences, a Canadian identity exists, and Puritanism is one of its defining terms.

The fiction of Westerners Margaret Laurence and Sinclair Ross shows that the attitudes which stem from historic Puritanism were by no means confined to Eastern Canada. Grandmother MacLeod, one of the main characters in Laurence's short story "To Set Our House in Order," is a stoic puritan who would fit perfectly into MacLennan's town of Grenville; and her dead husband, a doctor who was frustrated in his desire to be a classical scholar, is strikingly similar to Dr. Ainslie in *Each Man's Son*. Ross' powerful portrait of an unhappy clergyman in a small prairie town is an exposition of the puritan conscience. In his introduction to Ross' *As For Me and My House*, Roy Daniells writes: "The familiar furnishings of the Puritan soul materialize in these pages: standards, struggles, bleakness and tenacity, the horror of hypocrisy and of sexual sin, jealousy, the will of a jealous God, failure, the problem of fighting or flight, inexorable conscience, the slow realization of forgiveness, redemption and reconciliation after torments too long for any but the Puritan to endure."[7] The problem for many Canadians today is to redefine this religious heritage and separate the wheat from the chaff. Our study of the ambivalence in MacLennan's attitudes suggests that a simplistic denunciation of negative inhibitions as "puritan" is only the beginning, not the end, of the task.

In his analysis of English-Canadian and French-Canadian literary themes, Sutherland suggests that Canada has not had "an intellectual climate of positive myth and idealism to work within, as the Americans have had."[8] Canadian writers have not, that is to say, tended to make a naïve equation between Canadian existence and Eden, or the Promised Land. Indeed, the Puritan sense of the strength and reality of evil would militate against any such *naïvité*. There is, nevertheless, an idealistic myth in Canadian literature based on the land, seen as part of a Divine Order. MacLennan reveres the good land of Canada, and frequently uses it as an apocalyptic metaphor of the goal of man's quest. Cohen's myth is the holiness of the human body. MacLennan's attacks on life-styles of joyless negation, and Cohen's sexual mystique, are intimately related to the religious idealism and search for truth common to many works of Canadian literature.

Alan Ainslie and Bulstrode, in *Return of the Sphinx*, are as determined as their creator to hold this country together – with their bare hands, if necessary. MacLennan has always been an ardent nationalist, and his fiction will probably be seen by future historians as having played a part in our national survival. Here, as in his plea for saner attitudes towards sex, MacLennan was ahead of most of his fellow Canadians. By the sixties, nationalism in Canada was a rapidly growing force. Robert Fulford's suggestion, that very few Canadians have a commitment to the country as a whole, would have been more valid in 1961 than in 1971. Fulford writes: "In Canada a commitment like that, in an intellectual or an artist, would be considered gauche. In Russia a great man like Alexander Solzhenitsyn can say: 'For my entire life, I have had the soil of my homeland under my feet; only its pain do I hear, only about it do I write.' A Canadian who said anything equivalent would appear provincial and backward."[9] Well, gauche or not, MacLennan has been saying just this for some time. By 1972, he no longer seems to stand alone.[10]

MacLennan emphasizes that Canada is a youthful country. But as he has grown older, his fiction reflects a change in sympathetic alignment with youth and age. In his early novels, *Barometer Rising* and *Two Solitudes*, it is the youthful characters, such as Neil and Penny, Paul and Heather, who believe in Canada's destiny and embody it within themselves. They are opposed by an unsympathetic Old Guard. More recently, MacLennan has observed that many of today's youth do not value a united and independent country as much as he does. Hence the nationalist hero of his sixth novel is an older man near retirement, and MacLennan satirizes the idea of Youth summoning Age to the bar of TV justice.[11]

Cohen's fiction also has a nationalist bias. It is interesting to note that this is a more prominent motif in *Beautiful Losers* than in Cohen's first novel, published three years earlier. The 1966 novel specifically identifies a "dying America" with the four men who rape the thirteen-year-old Edith. Dying America is depicted as an aged King David, an impotent and decadent technological culture. And F.'s long letter to his friend speaks hyperbolically of bruising and destroying the American monolith. Nationalism is closely tied, in both Cohen and MacLennan, to their general idealism and moral stance. Cohen expressed to Michael Harris in 1969 his hope to see Canada become a "noble" rather than a powerful country.[12]

A constant theme in MacLennan's fiction is that the two founding cultures of Canada are ideally complementary and must "marry."

One of his fictional patterns depicts the Anglo-Saxon as the intellectual and morally serious puritan, while the French-Canadian supplies the gaiety, the *joie de vivre* which the Anglo-Saxon nature lacks: witness Alan Ainslie and Constance in *Return of the Sphinx*. In *Two Solitudes*, on the other hand, MacLennan emphasizes that the puritan element is found in the French as much as in the English. Father Beaubien is as puritan as Huntly McQueen. The narrative in both novels includes a symbolic marriage between French- and English-Canadians, a marriage which represents MacLennan's hope for a Canadian nation where the two cultures aid and nourish one another in a harmonius and loving relationship. His latest novel implies that this dream is still a possibility, but that time is fast running out.

When the two cultures marry and settle down together happily, the lost child may recover his home. Daniel likens all Québecois to linguistic and cultural orphans. It is ironic that he should accuse his father of not knowing what it means to be an orphan, for Alan Ainslie *is* an orphan. And so are we all, MacLennan insists, through rapid cultural change and the growth of technology. Cohen is with MacLennan in the attack on the dehumanizing influence of technology. Both authors stoutly defend the non-conforming individualist (Cohen's beautiful loser) against the social pressures designed to force him to conform. In our present technological society, animals are products and farms are factories. It is a short step from this to seeing men as products, and desirable social structures as those which maximize "rationality" and efficiency. Technology, in Ellul's analysis, drives relentlessly towards this state. Hence the attack on technology in the fiction of MacLennan and Cohen.

Like his fictional character Bruce Fraser, MacLennan has revolted far less than he has imagined. Perhaps there is a parallel here with Martin Luther, since both Luther and MacLennan failed to anticipate all the consequences of their revolt. MacLennan has bitterly attacked the negative and restrictive attitudes which stem from Puritan prohibitions. But the original prohibitions were based on values which MacLennan himself stoutly affirms and which many people in contemporary Canadian society now seem only too ready to reject.

He has attacked a misguided effort to earn salvation through work, but he holds no brief for idleness. He has attacked those who would condemn sex as evil, but his own attitude towards sex is eminently moral. He has attacked the "scurvy trick" which he claims has been played by the puritans in giving to the word "useful" such

a narrow meaning that beauty is excluded. He himself has restored
the original breadth of meaning to the word to make it include the
arts, which are useful to man in the highest sense. Granted this
wider meaning, MacLennan's emphasis on utility then becomes similar to that of the historic Puritans. He honours all things useful to
man in man's effort to live the good life. Preeminently, he honours
an affirmative morality based on love.[13]

In the last few decades, many Canadians have been discovering
and rediscovering the importance of beauty and the arts. Cohen's
Breavman or MacLennan's Dennis Morey would find it difficult today to get away with asking, "Is there art in Winnipeg?" Shizuye
Takashima, a Japanese-Canadian artist whose first book is based
on her experience of being imprisoned in Canada during World War
II, voices her impression of this new atmosphere thus: " 'I feel
there's a renaissance beginning in art in Canada. I can't understand
it. I was anti-Canadian – well, perhaps not anti so much as I never
felt at home here. . . . But when I went to New York, I began to see
Canada in a different way.' "[14] The "explosion" of creative writing
in Canada in the last two decades is another indication that Canadians agree with MacLennan's and Cohen's definition of utility as
including the arts.[15]

The pattern of death and rebirth found in all of MacLennan's
novels points to the religious nature of the vision which underlies
his work. The hero of *Barometer Rising* is described on several
occasions as a man returned from the dead. Neil MacRae has been
wounded in the war and has spent some time in hospitals – a "phan-
tasmal," lonely existence. His shell-shock leaves him mentally exhausted. Alone in Halifax, Neil thinks that he is like a dead man,
totally unable to communicate with other human beings. Neil exists
in a purgatorial state. His hatred for his uncle and his desire for
revenge take precedence over all other feelings. Penny realizes that
Neil is being "killed by the burden in his mind." (*BR* 109) The
physical shock of the harbour explosion reverses the effect of Neil's
original shell-shock. He survives, and suddenly realizes that he feels
fine. In the subsequent work of caring for the wounded, Neil loses
his feeling of hatred for Wain even before he discovers his dead
body. Neil is reborn when his personal problems cease to occupy
him in the face of the general suffering. Purged of hatred and reunited with Penny, Neil faces the future with confidence.

In *Two Solitudes*, the death-rebirth pattern is worked out through
two people, father and son. For Athanase Tallard, there is no rebirth in this world. His life is described by McQueen as a tragedy,

that of being caught between two stools all his life. Held within the straight-jacket of his own nature, Athanase fights and defeats himself. His emotions and his mind are irreconcilable. With his mind, Athanase is attracted to science and to rationalism. He sees Mcqueen's plan for a factory in Saint-Marc as the key to remodelling and improving the village. But with his emotions Athanase is tied to the land, to his French people and the Roman Catholic religion: "Although he professed to respect little but logic and mental brilliance, Athanase sensed a peculiar power in the priest." (*TS* 128) The two sides of Athanase's nature thus reflect what MacLennan depicts as the dominating aspects of the two main Canadian cultures. The deep split within Athanase leads him to failure and ruin. In the experience of his son, Paul, MacLennan shows the resolution of the conflicts. With the aid of an English school, the bilingual Paul is able to unify in himself the opposing tendencies which ruined his father. When Paul reappears after five years at sea, he is a whole man, strong and confident.

Stephen Lassiter's period of acute depression and loneliness during the climactic scenes in *The Precipice* are also shown as a kind of death. In a small New York café, Stephen listens to the music of Povey Bartt and feels that it represents all the loneliness and longing in the world. The music is identified with the American Dream – and the failure of that dream. Alone in Chicago, bitter, jobless and filled with self-contempt, Stephen's suffering is acute. There is no actual rebirth for Stephen within the novel, only the hint that this may be possible when Stephen is willing to accept himself and to accept Lucy's love.

Daniel Ainslie's death and rebirth in *Each Man's Son* has been described in Chapter Six. After passing through a spiritual wasteland, Ainslie comes to accept both himself and others, and with this new acceptance he is free to love. His lesson is similar to that which George Stewart learns in *The Watch*: "Except a corn of wheat fall into the ground and die, it abideth alone: but if it die, it bringeth forth much fruit. . . ." Both men learn that they must die to their desires to dominate or possess another person, die to their attempts to live through another person, and die to their fear of life. In the new Jerome, triumphantly returned from the dead, MacLennan shows what man is capable of when he has died to himself and lives for other men and for "the mystery our ancestors confidently called God." The death-rebirth pattern recurs in *Return of the Sphinx*, in the experience of Alan Ainslie.

The rebirth pattern in MacLennan's fiction thus suggests a paral-

lel with Christian theology, a humanistic version which closely resembles the Christian belief in the death and resurrection of Christ,
and the necessity for our sharing in both this death and new life.
MacLennan's version emphasizes immanence, while traditional
Christianity affirms the immanence in man and nature of a transcen-
dent God. MacLennan seems to object to the word "sin," because
of its association with guilt, which he sees as a neurotic fear or
death-force. Nevertheless, MacLennan is very much aware of human failings such as pride and self-will which destroy human happiness and even life itself. He is evangelistic in showing the necessity
for dying to these failings. Many of his characters are in search of
a God, and some of those whom he depicts most sympathetically
(such as old Dr. Dougald MacKenzie, Captain Yardley and Matt
McCunn) remain Presbyterians for life. Matt's original faith in
people's innocence seems to have been changed by his war experiences, which he terms a liberal education. He says that these experiences turned him into a Presbyterian again, "for if original sin don't
account for what goes on there, nothing else does."

An incident such as we find in *Return of the Sphinx*, where the
teenager Constance is initiated into the art of physical love-making
by her uncle, would never have appeared in MacLennan's fiction in
the forties. In general, MacLennan's treatment of sex is more casual
in his last two novels. But only in *The Watch That Ends the Night*
does he tend to treat sex as something rather unimportant. This attitude is not found in either his earlier novels or his sixth one, *Return
of the Sphinx*. There is also the tendency, in *The Watch,* to make a
rigid separation between sex and love, whereas the moral attitude
would normally link them together. Sex is so easy, Catherine tells
George, but love is exhausting; sex is morally neutral, Jerome says,
"unless it's connected with cruelty." (*WE* 162) MacLennan is
identifying sex with the physical body and love with the immaterial
spirit and opting, here, for the spirit. The dualist tendency inherent
in the ending of this novel has been discussed in Chapter Nine. In
"The Future of the Novel as an Art Form," an address given in
1959 at the Golden Jubilee of the University of Saskatchewan, Mac-
Lennan said: "The fact that the human body was kept out of love
by the Victorians seems an inadequate reason for keeping the soul
out of it today." (*SR* 157) In this address, given in the same year
as the publication of *The Watch*, MacLennan attacks the "automatic cynicism" which he finds in many contemporary novels, and
suggests that the serious reader would welcome a more spiritual or

moral approach. The form of his attack suggests a latent tension in his mind between body and soul, matter and spirit.

MacLennan's ambivalent attitude towards work might be explained by the same dualistic tendency. If it is only the things of the spirit that have ultimate reality, then the things of the world can be dismissed as of no importance, and the urge to reform material evils by action can be condemned as materialistic. In condemning action, I suggest that MacLennan has lost sight of something which is basic to the Christian tradition. Christian theologians, from St. Augustine to Sören Kierkegaard, have understood that knowledge of the good is insufficient in itself without the determination to act upon that knowledge. To live as a Christian means *to strive*. The active life is itself an expression of spirit. In his novels, MacLennan affirms this part of his religious heritage through the actions and ideals of all his major protagonists. Yet many of his essays condemn action as materialistic and puritanical.

The attack upon action as materialistic is more direct in the essays, although the idea is latent in much of his fiction. In "Cross Country," he attacks action as a "materialistic panacea of the puritans," (*CC* 86) and blames puritanism for conditioning its members to act rather than to think. In " 'Help Thou Mine Unbelief,' " another essay in the same 1949 collection, MacLennan writes:

Religion can never be anything save a thing of the spirit. Its values are of the spirit, its aims are of the spirit. But the society in which we live has become so increasingly materialistic that even our standards of goodness are generally materialistic ones. . . . Today a man's goodness is measured – at least in the non-Catholic world, by his material services to his fellow man. . . . Man, not God, is the master who must be served. The present human world, *not the divine external world*, is the one which counts. (*CC* 139–40, italics mine)

The divorce of matter and spirit is quite clear in this quotation and is so throughout the essay. The world and the body are abandoned as unimportant, and religious values are relegated exclusively to the realm of the spirit.

In a postscript to this essay, MacLennan writes: "It seems to me a tragic situation, after so many centuries of union, that the Greco-Christian civilization should split into its two original parts, rational humanism and uncritical faith, and that we should be asked to choose between them. There is no reason why the mystical approach to a vision of God – the approach followed by Jesus Himself – should be incompatible with modern scientific discoveries." (*CC* 153) MacLennan gives a strange twist, here, to the components of the

Graeco-Christian civilization, which I suggest might be described more accurately as rational humanism and mysticism, rather than "rational humanism and uncritical faith." The traditional Christian faith in the Incarnation provides the synthesis of rational humanism and mysticism, a synthesis which is broken by the Manichaean disregard for the body and the material world. In " 'Help Thou Mine Unbelief,' " MacLennan says that the stupendous achievement of the early Christian Church consisted in "the link it contrived to forge between the conception of God and the conception of Jesus Christ." (*CC* 146) The key word here is "contrived." If the link is merely artificial or theoretical, the original Christian faith will tend to separate again into rational humanism and mysticism. We see this process at work in the writings of MacLennan as he wrestles with the meaning of life, spirit, body, world. His rational humanism leads him to suggest that we must look to the scientists for the new symbols of a religion which will be acceptable to the modern intellectual, and that "we can at least do our best to live earthly lives in accordance with the ethics of Jesus Christ." (*CC* 148) His mysticism tends to repudiate all this as shadowy, unreal, unimportant.

I am not suggesting that this dualistic tendency dominates MacLennan's fiction. It plays a major part only in the final part of *The Watch That Ends the Night*. I do feel, however, that it is latent in his writing in connection with his attack on puritanism, and that it may help to provide an explanation for the ambivalence in his attitudes towards work, sex, beauty and pleasure. The two components of pre-Christian civilization, rational humanism and mysticism, remain unresolved in MacLennan's novels. His attention to ethical values, many of which are common to rational humanism and Christianity, is more obvious than his tendency towards mysticism. MacLennan's fiction reflects the same overriding concern with morality which we find in his essays.

Although MacLennan's emphasis, like that of the historic Puritans, is primarily moral and intellectual, there is an element of mysticism in his essays and his novels. The death-rebirth pattern experienced by his protagonists is mystical, as is the glorification of the doctor as a person with almost supernatural healing powers. There is also a feeling of reverence for life which might be described as mystical. This figures most prominently in *The Watch That Ends the Night* and, to a lesser extent, in *Two Solitudes* and *Return of the Sphinx*. In *The Watch*, the mysticism is to be found in MacLennan's reverent attitude towards the vital life-force which is in Catherine and Jerome Martell. Catherine, in her gallant fight against illness, is described as a flame in the dark, and Jerome strikes George as being more a force of nature than a man. MacLennan speaks of this thing which he feels to be the ultimate reality as "spirit" and "Life-Force," and he summarizes the whole story of *The Watch* as a conflict between his spirit and the human condition. George says that he has recognized an immense amount of this force in people who might be judged, by their actions, to be bad; and sometimes very little of it in others who appear to be good. The force is amoral: "This mysterious thing, which creates, destroys and recreates, is the sole force which equals the merciless fate binding a human being to his mortality." (*WE* 341) There is, however, a moral aspect to this amoral life-force. Jerome's vitality overflows so as to help those around him. He wants to help people get the most out of what life they have.

In *Two Solitudes*, a similar mysticism is presented through Yardley's reveries. Once, Yardley had spent one whole afternoon at sea watching some fish beside the ship. The memory of their beauty and apparent aimlessness never left him. He thinks that knowledge is like a curtain drawn across the mind to conceal from us a mystery too awful to be faced. As Yardley is dying, he thinks of the beauty and mystery of the world, and of the infinite pleasure which a man could find in the lines of a single vase: "He had been ashamed then of liking useless things which were merely beautiful, for he had been given a strict upbringing." He now feels the wonder of the world around him and within: the wonder of life, seen through microscope and telescope and with the naked eye. His mood and attitude as death overtakes him is one of reverent wonder and thankfulness. In Yardley's reverence, however, there is no suspicion directed against material things, no preference for spirit over matter; his last movement is an effort to see the robin feeding its young. With this difference, then, the mood is similar to that which dominates the closing pages of *The Watch*. Life is a gift, to be accepted with joyful gratitude. In the final pages of *Return of the Sphinx*, Ainslie is restored to joy, almost to life, by his mystic kinship with the vast land ("this loveliness that nobody could understand or possess") for which he thanks God.

This attitude provides the link between MacLennan's mysticism and his moral seriousness. MacLennan sees man as being under a *moral* obligation to appreciate the *mystical* gift of life, and to respond fully to the opportunities to love. The puritanism which he is attacking seems to value denial for its own sake. But historic Puritanism taught that denial or death may be part of life. The Puritan was aware, like Daniel Ainslie, that life is never so vivid as when it is endangered, "nor was a human being ever so vitally himself as when he had passed through pain and emerged on the other side of it." (*EMS* 85) In the death of Mollie MacNeil and the suffering of Catherine Stewart, MacLennan shows that death and suffering may be redemptive for others. In the rebirth-through-death experiences of Neil MacRae, Daniel Ainslie, Jerome Martell and Alan Ainslie, he shows that man must die in order to live.

Cohen's fiction has the same blend of morality and mysticism, but the element of mysticism is more prominent. His sense of the holiness of the entire natural creation reflects a growing awareness in Western society that man's "dominion" over the world was never intended to mean the power to pollute and destroy indiscriminately. Not all ecologists and anti-pollutionists are mystics, but a reverence for the natural order which is mystic in its inspiration and its basis underlies the desire to protect the quality of our environment.

Cohen's belief in the unity of body and soul, of the oneness of the human being in himself and with his world, is clear in both *The Favorite Game* and *Beautiful Losers*. When "the word is made flesh," as Cohen phrases it in the opening section of his first novel, a scar happens. The embodied spirit becomes subject to love, loss and death. But this is what life is all about, Cohen says. Man and his world form the "shit glory tree." Lameness is an aspect of perfection, and weeds are flowers that no one collects. This is the "all diamond" stance which aligns Cohen, that iconoclastic moralist, with twentieth-century mystics such as Patrick White and Teilhard de Chardin, and with the ancient Jewish cabala. Don't be ashamed, Urine says, in the fantasy where the materials covering Edith's navel speak out. And don't be ashamed, Cohen is saying, of the body or its acts. He pictures the body as a telephone or communication system connecting one human being with another – and with himself. To love is to lose. To live is to fail.

Certainly Canadians have had more than their share of "baggy failures" in the past. Writing of the Jewish community in Canada, Rabbi Stuart Rosenberg notes that the age-old Jewish struggle to draw success out of failure has a general parallel in the shorter Canadian experience. He quotes an unidentified observer to the effect that the Canadian character is marked by the knowledge of failure.[16] In an essay entitled "The Canadian Character," Mac-Lennan makes the same point. The three founding groups of this nation, French, Loyalist and Highland Scots, "became Canadians because the nations or factions to which they had belonged had suffered total defeat in war. It was in their response to the challenge of these three separate defeats, a response which in each case was remarkably similar, that the common denominator in the Canadian character was forged." (*CC* 10) Yet the past, as F. advises his friends, is joyously prophetic, and possibility surrounds us "on this cargo deck of wide labels." A people shaped in such a forge are not easily discouraged. But the land is still in the process of being born. MacLennan phrases it poetically in his centennial tribute to the nation: "This is a land that can best be described in music, but the music to describe it has yet to be written."[17]

The novels of Leonard Cohen and Hugh MacLennan celebrate life. In one of MacLennan's essays, he writes of the novel's power to become an active agent within a society, to make social situations live, to put flesh and blood on political and economic forces. Again one is reminded of D.H. Lawrence whose tone, like Cohen's and MacLennan's, is often evangelistic. In *Lady Chatterley's Lover,* Lawrence's narrator comments on the importance of the way in which our sympathy flows and recoils: "And here lies the vast importance of the novel, properly handled. It can inform and lead into new places the flow of our sympathetic consciousness, and it can lead our sympathy away in recoil from things gone dead."

MacLennan intends to lead our sympathy away from a negative, death-like fear of beauty and joy, and from guilt feelings which inhibit us from living and loving. To these negative attitudes he has given the name of puritanism. MacLennan's own novels, however, are proof that the moral values of the seventeenth-century Puritans are far from dead. Cohen takes another tack in the war against Canadian inhibitions: shock treatment. The bawdy eroticism of *Beautiful Losers* comes across, to many Canadians, as just that. The Argentinian sex orgy episode is a perfect example of Cohen's iconoclastic moralism and his consciously paradoxical stance. The prophetic role is mocked, here, as self-indulgence, while at the same time the prophecy, the social criticism, is intended to be taken seriously:

> Change! Purify! Experiment! Cauterize! Reverse! Burn! Preserve! Teach!
> . . . All I had in the wrecked world was a needle and thread, so I got down on my knees, I pulled pieces out of the mess and I started to stitch them together. . . . All I heard was pain, all I saw was mutilation. My needle going so madly, sometimes I found I'd run the thread right through my own flesh and I was joined to one of my own creations – I'd rip us apart – and then I heard my own voice howling with the others, and I knew that I was also truly part of the disaster. (*BL* 175)

F.'s compassion costs him his "hard-on" and, in the outrageous comedy which follows, the Danish Vibrator takes over the structured chaos. Truth and fun. Or call it a comic version of Kierkegaard's definition of the truth as subjectivity. The artist-prophet is fully involved in humanity's weaknesses, failures and struggles, not above or beyond these in calm superiority.

Here is the creative iconoclasm which every culture needs. The fiction of Cohen and MacLennan, like that of the earlier iconoclast D.H. Lawrence, is essentially moral. It poses the artist in his traditional role as teacher, prophet, seer, impatient reformer, Dr. Frankenstein with a deadline. Cohen uses the Indian myth of Oscotarach as a metaphor of the function of art. The Huron Indians believed that Oscotarach, the Head-Piercer, cleansed the skulls of all who went by, as a necessary preparation for immortality. (*BL* 184) Cohen's F. hopes to perform a similar function for the reader: "The surgery is deep in progress, darling. I am with you." We may not be immortal when Cohen and MacLennan get through with us, but we should be gayer, wiser and considerably less inhibited.

NOTES

1. See C.S. Lewis, *The Screwtape Letters* (Glasgow: Fontana, 1942), p. 55.

2. See Northrop Frye, *The Bush Garden: Essays on the Canadian Imagination* (Toronto: Anansi, 1971), Preface, pp. i-iii. One example which Frye gives of imaginative forms common to all of Canada is a perception of colour based on the pattern of four seasons. In an exhibition of paintings done by undergraduate students, Frye was at a loss to analyse the differences in imaginative qualities in a painting done by a student from Ghana: "I finally realized what it was: he had lived, in his impressionable years, in a world where colour was a constant datum: he had never seen colour as a cycle that got born in spring, matured in a burst of autumn flame, and then died out into a largely abstract, black and white world."

3. See *Reminiscences and Incidents of the Reverend John Anderson*, ed. by his son J.D. Anderson (Toronto: William Briggs, 1910). This striking portrait of a Presbyterian clergyman in Ontario in the latter part of the nineteenth century might well have been titled "An Autobiography of a Puritan." It shows how recently moral and religious attitudes dominated every phase of life in this part of Canada.

4. Max Ferguson, CBC radio, March 26, 1971.

5. Jack Batten, "Cohen: he's so good at everything he does," *Globe and Mail*, December 9, 1970.

6. See Ronald Sutherland, "Twin Solitudes," *Canadian Literature*, No. 31 (Winter 1967), 5-23, and *Second Image: Comparative Studies in Quebec/Canadian Literature* (Toronto: New Press, 1971). In "Twin Solitudes," p. 6, Sutherland writes: "It also becomes evident, interestingly enough,

that a good number of the accepted differences between the cultures of French Canada and English Canada do not in fact exist"; and p. 22: "If the notable parallels in French-Canadian and English-Canadian Literature have any significance at all, then it must be because there does exist a single, common national mystique, a common set of conditioning forces, the mysterious apparatus of a single sense of identity."

7. Sinclair Ross, *As For Me and My House*, NCL 4 (Toronto: McClelland and Stewart, 1957). Introduction by Roy Daniells, p. vii. See also Robert Fulford, "Face-Off: movie for 11-year-olds; book for dirty old men," *Ottawa Citizen*, December 4, 1971, p. 32: "Canadian culture, French as well as English, suffers from Puritan inhibitions and these affect even those writers who believe they have long since cast off the religions which gave force to those inhibitions." Fulford is using the term in MacLennan's negative sense.

8. Ronald Sutherland, "Twin Solitudes," *Canadian Literature*, No. 31, p. 23.

9. Robert Fulford, "Canadians no real emotional sense of country's size," *Ottawa Citizen*, October 30, 1971, p. 32.

10. See John Doig, " 'Keep it Canadian' – the nationalists are gaining," *The Toronto Daily Star*, December 4, 1971, p. 17: "Today, a movement called the Committee for an Independent Canada is in the vanguard of a battle to save the country from another, more insidious, invasion: The gradual takeover of its economy and its culture by the United States. . . . Since its quiet birth in September last year, the committee has ridden on a rising swell of popular nationalism. Its followers are now numbered in the thousands."

11. Cf. Hugh MacLennan, "Two Solitudes that Meet and Greet in Hope and Hate," *Maclean's*, August 1971, p. 50, where MacLennan records the words of a visiting poet from France at the beginning of the sixties. The poet claims the current English-French cordiality in Montreal is only between people of MacLennan's age: " 'I'm talking about the new generation. They hate you. They hate the Church. You won't be able to control them. Nobody will be able to control them.' " Later in the same article, MacLennan writes that most French-Canadians over the age of thirty-five are now more strongly federal than ever, "even in their feelings," but that Radio-Canada and many French-Canadian students are separatist. See also Hugh MacLennan, "Murder of Truth . . . Murder of people," *Montreal Gazette*, November 21, 1970, p. 7: "Our present unity is mostly a unity of people over thirty; on the executive level, of people over 40." Cf. Alec Lucas, *Hugh MacLennan*, p. 47: "MacLennan stood with youth on the ramparts of the generation gap until *Return of the Sphinx*, when he left his position to cross over to the middle-aged."

12. See Note 7, Chapter Seven.

13. Cf. Peter Buitenhuis, *Hugh MacLennan* (Toronto: Forum House, 1969), p. 9: "The Presbyterian in MacLennan may account not only for his Christian idealism but also for the strain of moralism found in his work."

14. Kay Kritzwiser, "Colourful recall in an artist's book," *The Globe and Mail*, September 11, 1971.

15. See George Woodcock, "Swarming of Poets," *Canadian Literature*, No. 50 (Autumn 1971), p. 3. Woodcock writes that when *Canadian Literature*

began in 1959 he promised himself that every published novel and book of verse would be reviewed there. In 1959 there were twenty-four volumes of poetry. But by 1971, "the poetry explosion of the past decades . . . was going bang in my face. Last year, according to *Canadian Literature*'s annual checklist, more than 120 collections of verse in English alone were published in Canada. . . . This year . . . the total may well run into 250 or 300 titles in English."

16. See Stuart E. Rosenberg, *The Jewish Community in Canada*, Vol. II, In the Midst of Freedom (Toronto: McClelland and Stewart, 1971), p. 9.

17. *Colour of Canada*, text by Hugh MacLennan, the Canadian Illustrated Library (Toronto: McClelland and Stewart, 1967), p. 86.

INDEX